BIG-NOTE PIANO
CHART HITS
OF 2016–2017

ISBN 978-1-4950-9091-2

HAL•LEONARD®

7777 W. BLUEMOUND RD. P.O. BOX 13819 MILWAUKEE, WI 53213

Visit Hal Leonard Online at
www.halleonard.com

CONTENTS

BLUE AIN'T YOUR COLOR

Words and Music by HILLARY LINDSEY,
STEVEN LEE OLSEN and CLINT LAGERBERG

Moderately

I can see you o-ver there, star-ing at your drink, watch-ing that ice sink all a-lone to-night. And chanc-es are you're sit-ting here in this bar 'cause he ain't gon-na treat you right. Well, it's

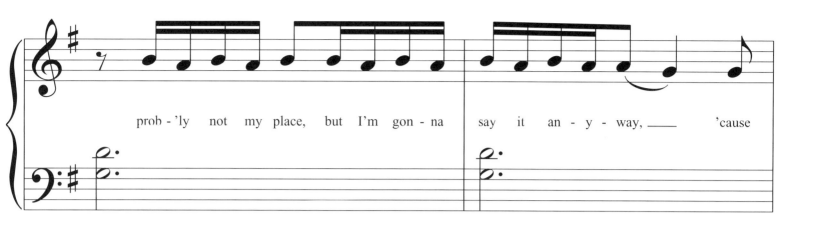

prob - 'ly not my place, but I'm gon - na say it an - y - way, ___ 'cause

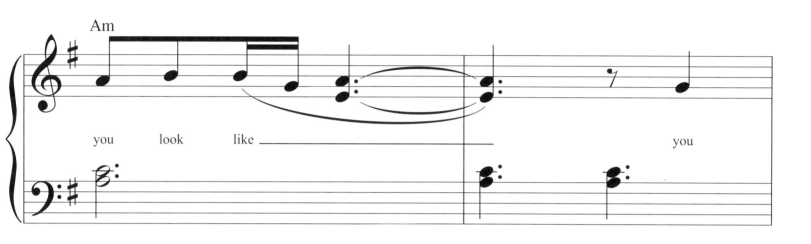

you look like _____ you

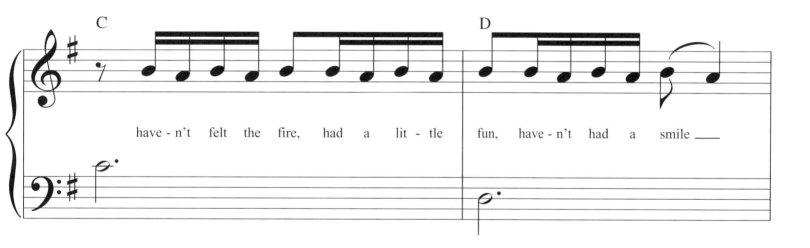

have - n't felt the fire, had a lit - tle fun, have - n't had a smile ___

in a lit - tle while, ___ ba - by.

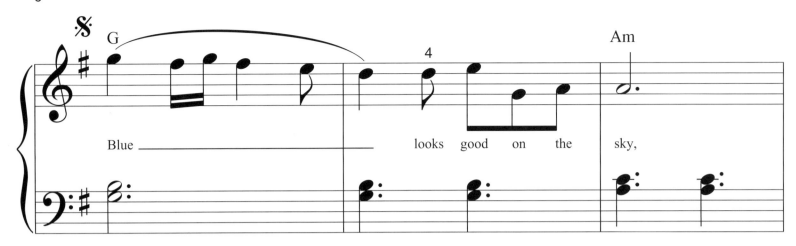

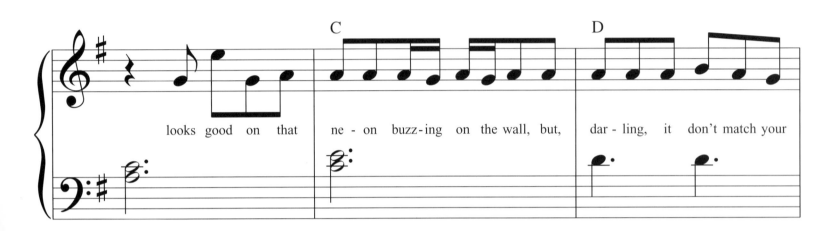

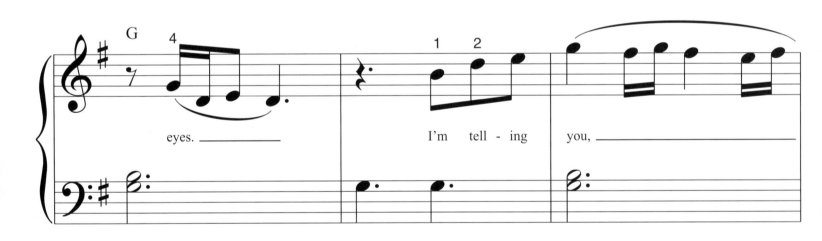

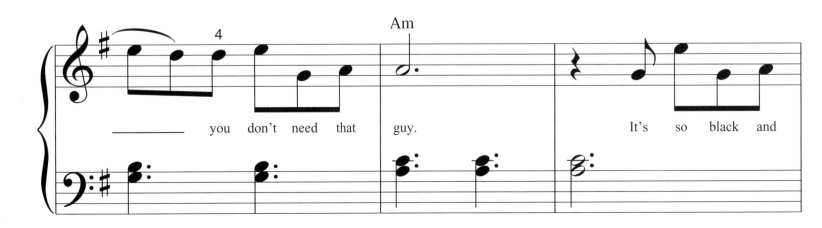

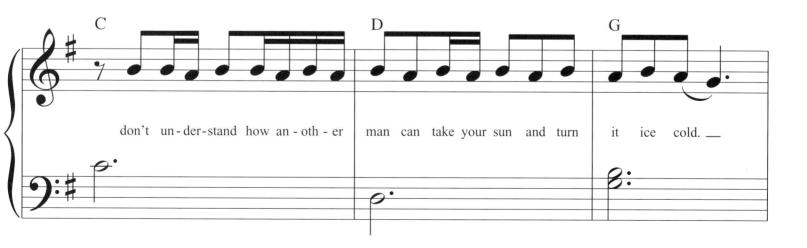

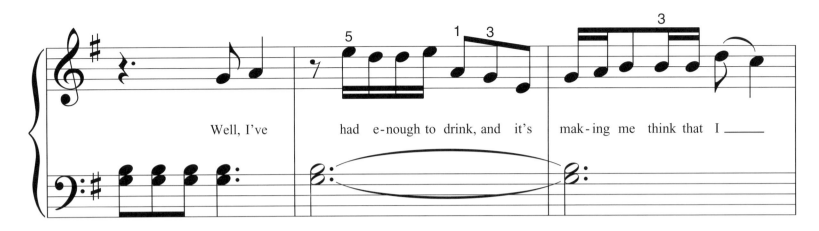

Well, I've had e-nough to drink, and it's mak-ing me think that I _____

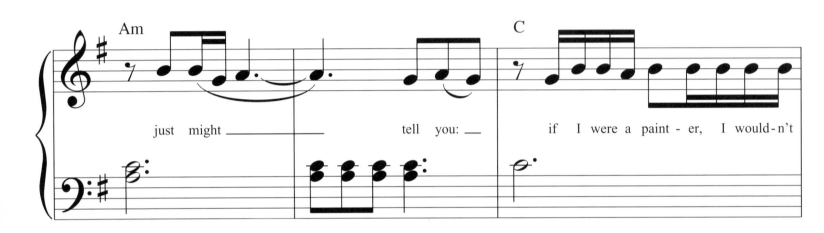

just might _____ tell you: _____ if I were a paint - er, I would-n't

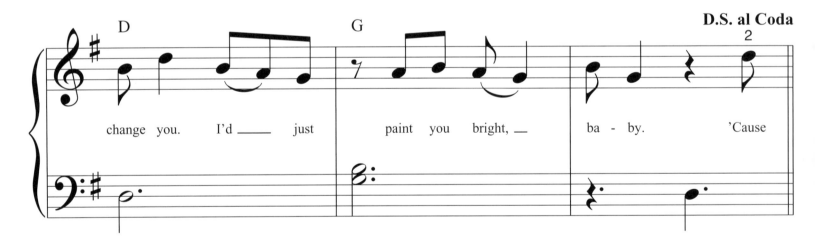

change you. I'd _____ just paint you bright, _____ ba - by. 'Cause

D.S. al Coda

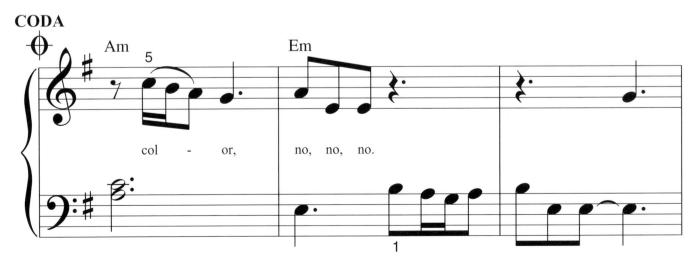

CODA

col - or, no, no, no.

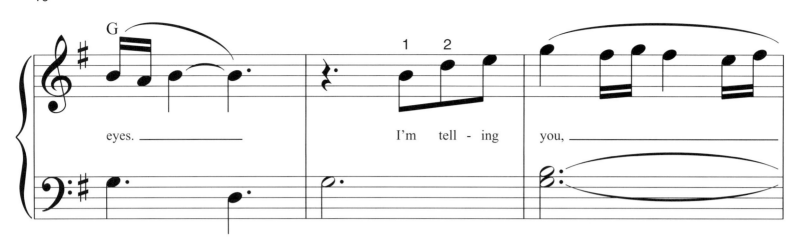

eyes. _____ I'm tell - ing you, _____

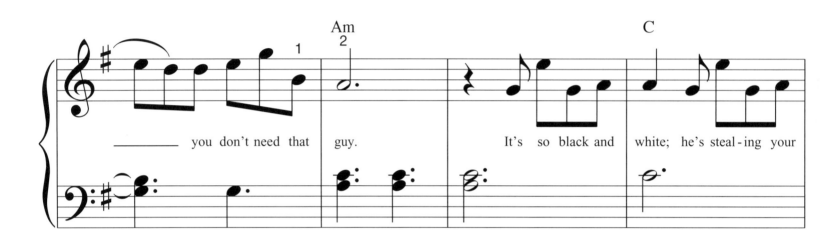

_____ you don't need that guy. It's so black and white; he's steal - ing your

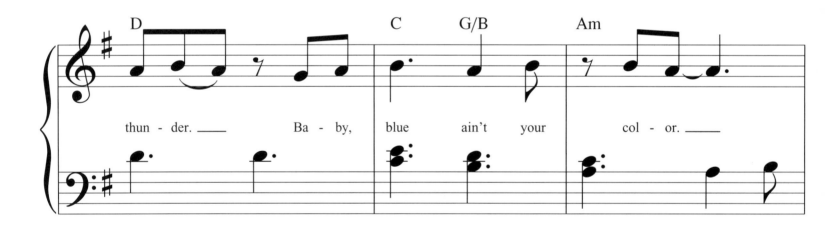

thun - der. _____ Ba - by, blue ain't your col - or. _____

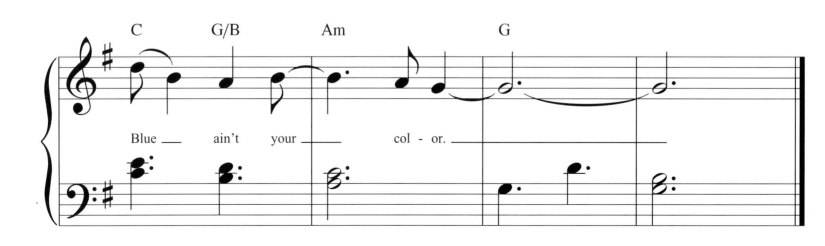

Blue _____ ain't your _____ col - or. _____

LET ME LOVE YOU

Words and Music by JUSTIN BIEBER, CARL ROSEN,
WILLIAM GRIGAHCINE, EDWIN PEREZ, TEDDY MENDEZ,
ANDREW WOTMAN, ALEXANDRA TAMPOSI, LOUIS BELL,
LUMIDEE CEDENO, BRIAN LEE and STEVEN MARSDEN

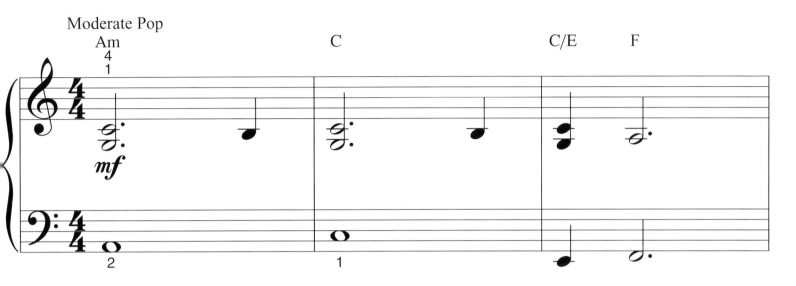

I used to be-lieve we were
sleep at the

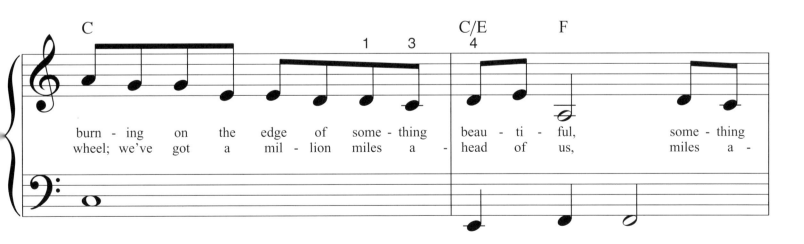

burn-ing on the edge of some-thing beau-ti-ful, some-thing
wheel; we've got a mil-lion miles a-head of us, miles a-

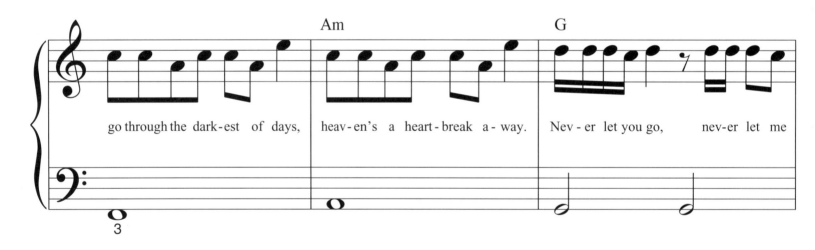

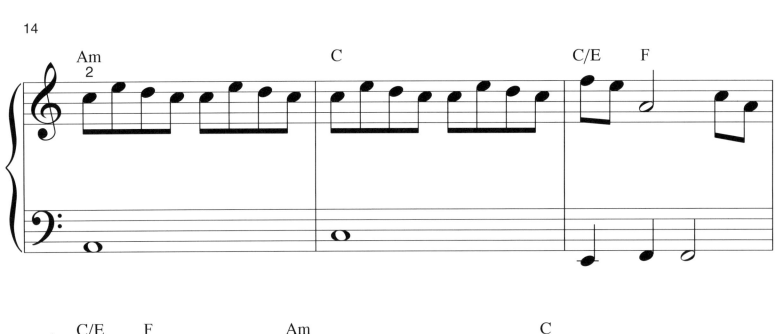

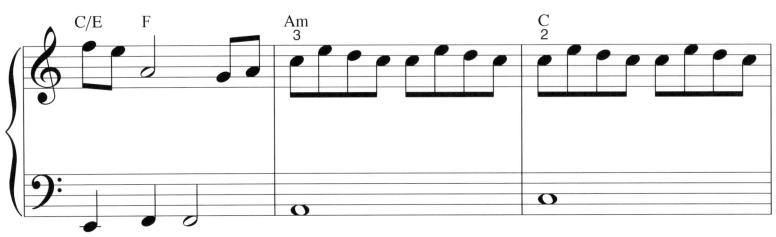

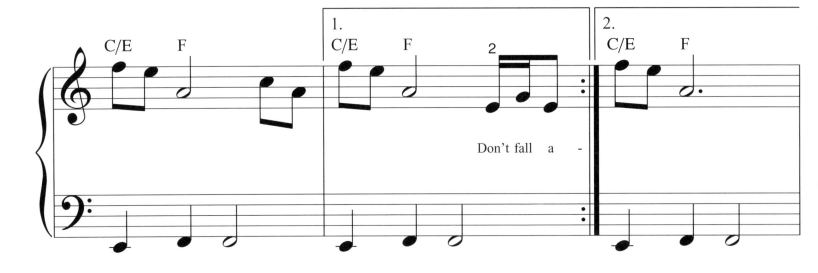

Don't fall a -

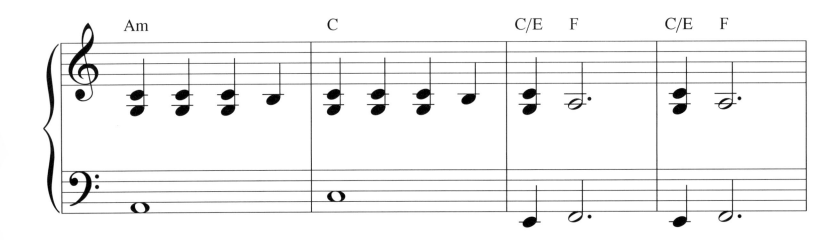

CLOSER

Words and Music by ANDREW TAGGART,
ISAAC SLADE, JOSEPH KING, ASHLEY FRANGIPANE,
SHAUN FRANK and FREDERIC KENNETT

Moderate groove

mf

Hey,   I was do-ing just   fine be-fore I met you. I drink too
You   look — as   good as the day I met you. — I for-

much and that's an is-sue but I'm o-kay.
get just why I left you. I was in-sane.

Hey,   yeah, tell your   friends it was nice to meet them, but I
Stay,   and play that   Blink One-Eight-y-Two song that we

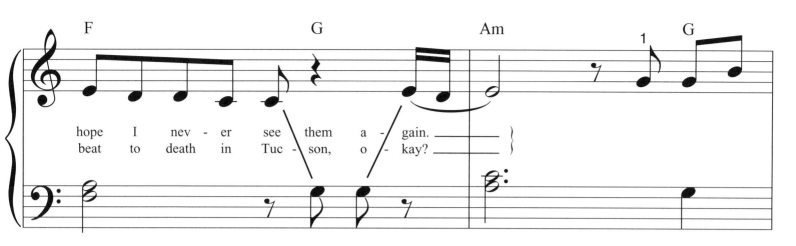

hope I nev - er see them a - gain.
beat to death in Tuc - son, o - kay?

I know it breaks your heart; moved to the cit - y in a broke - down car and,

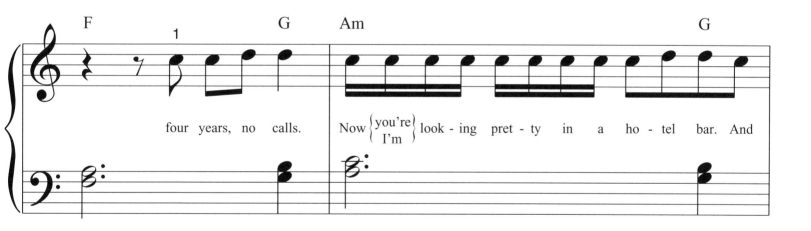

four years, no calls. Now {you're / I'm} look - ing pret - ty in a ho - tel bar. And

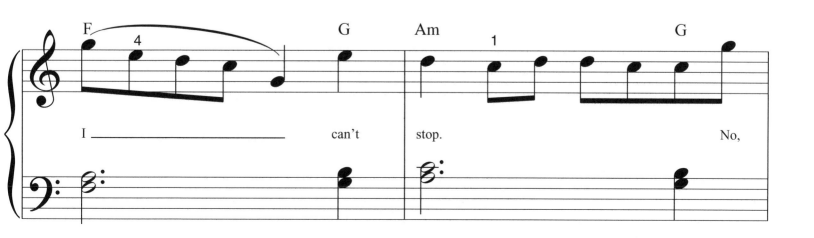

I _____ can't stop. No,

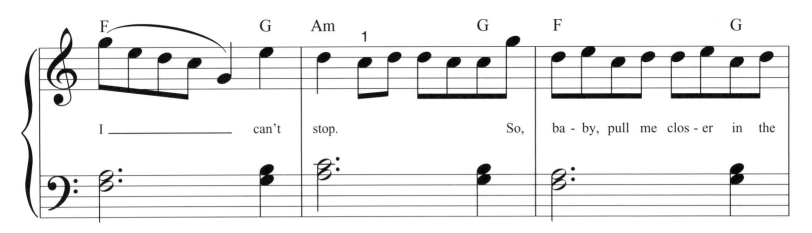

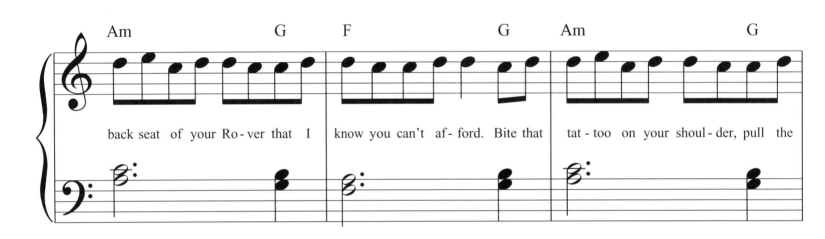

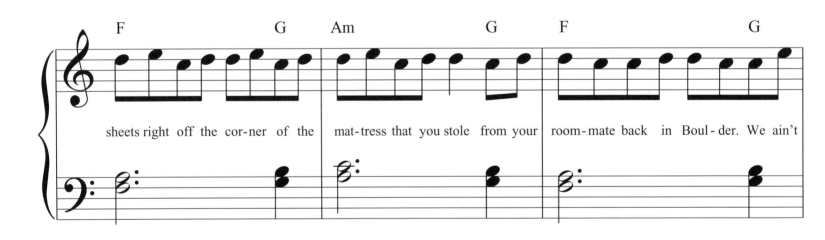

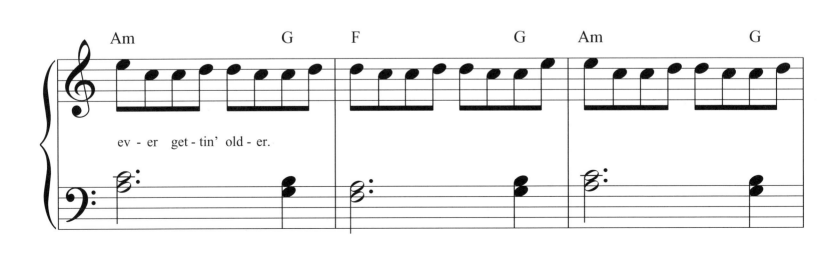

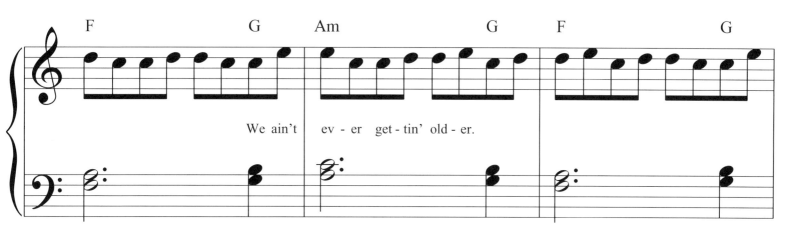

We ain't ev - er get-tin' old - er.

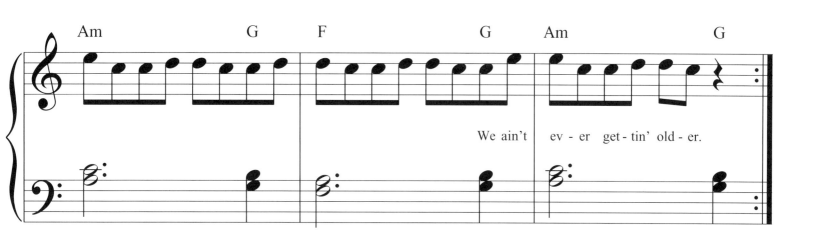

We ain't ev - er get-tin' old - er.

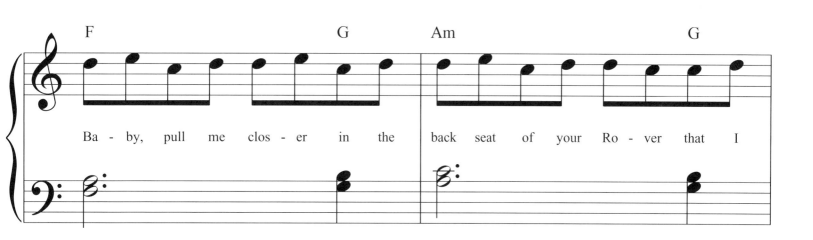

Ba - by, pull me clos - er in the back seat of your Ro - ver that I

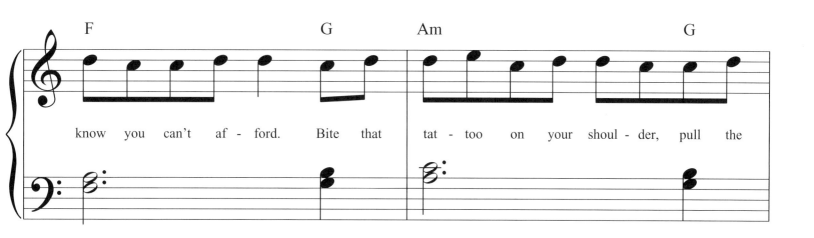

know you can't af - ford. Bite that tat - too on your shoul - der, pull the

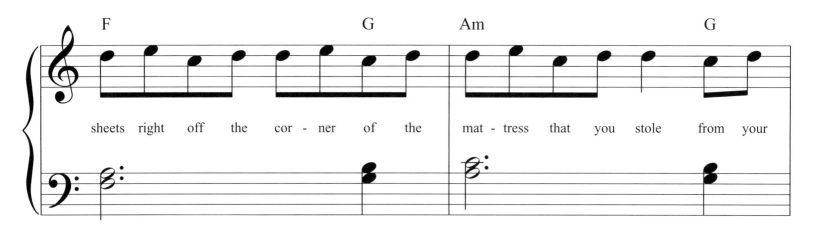

sheets right off the cor - ner of the mat - tress that you stole from your

room - mate back in Boul - der. We ain't ev - er get - tin' old - er. We ain't

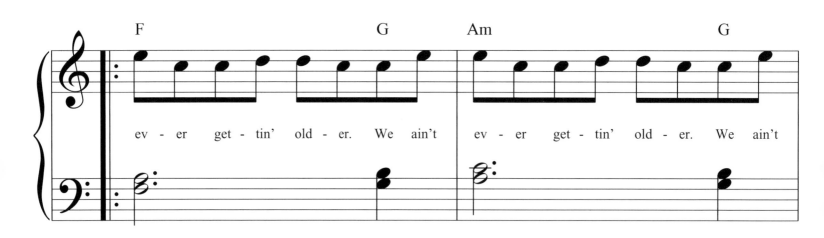

ev - er get - tin' old - er. We ain't ev - er get - tin' old - er. We ain't

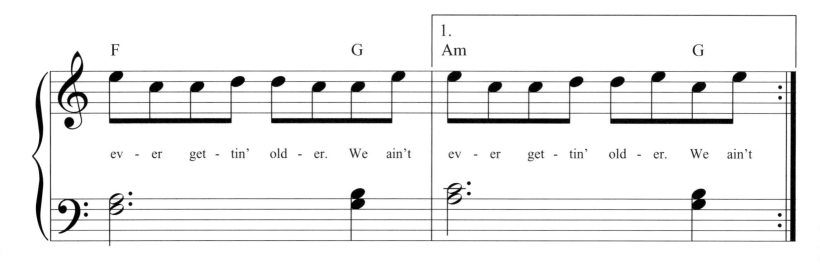

ev - er get - tin' old - er. We ain't ev - er get - tin' old - er. We ain't

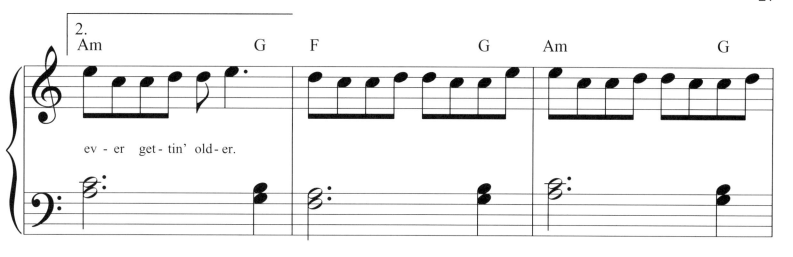

ev - er get - tin' old - er.

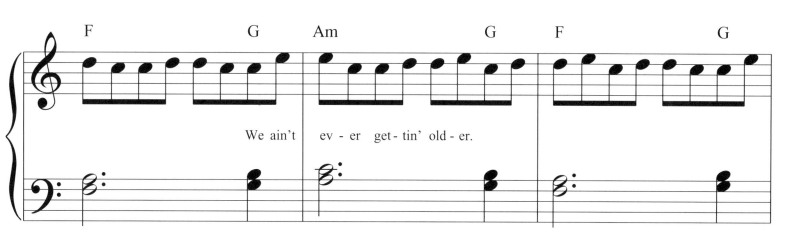

We ain't ev - er get - tin' old - er.

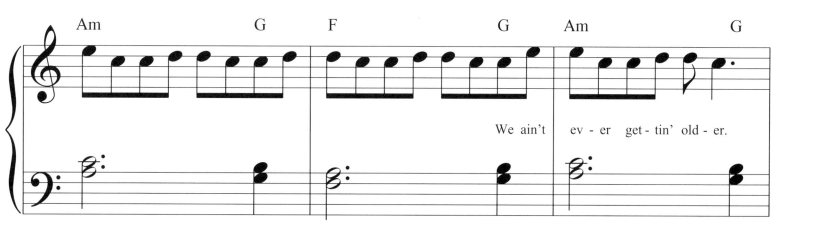

We ain't ev - er get - tin' old - er.

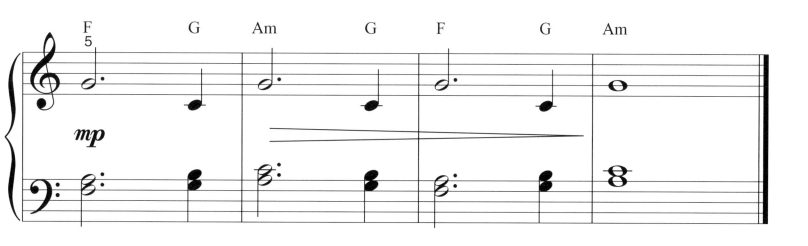

COLD WATER

Words and Music by THOMAS PENTZ, KAREN ØRSTED,
HENRY ALLEN, JUSTIN BIEBER, BENJAMIN LEVIN,
ED SHEERAN, JAMIE SCOTT and PHILIP MECKSEPER

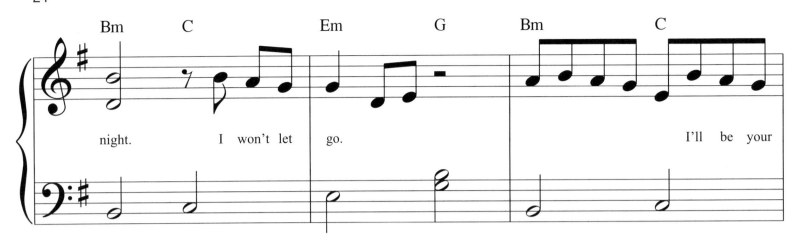

night.   I won't let   go.   I'll be your

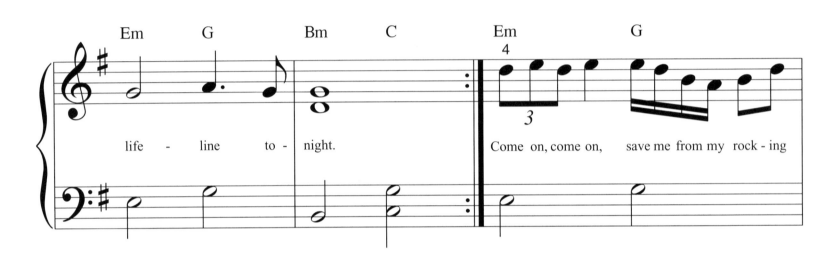

life - line   to - night.   Come on, come on,   save me from my rock - ing

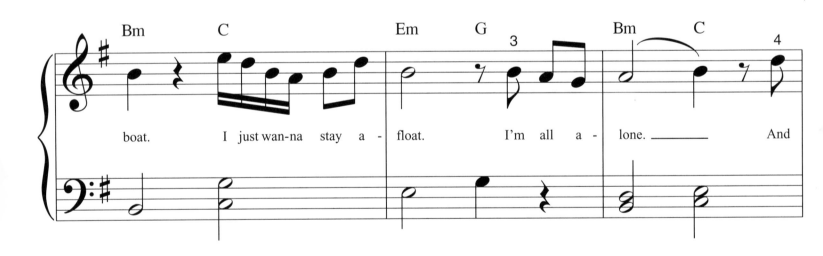

boat.   I just wan-na stay a - float.   I'm all a -   lone. _____   And

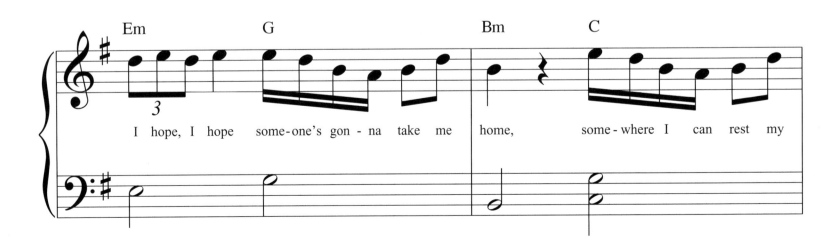

I hope, I hope some-one's gon - na take me   home,   some - where I can rest my

soul. I need to know _____ you won't let go.

I'll be your life - line to - night. You won't let go.

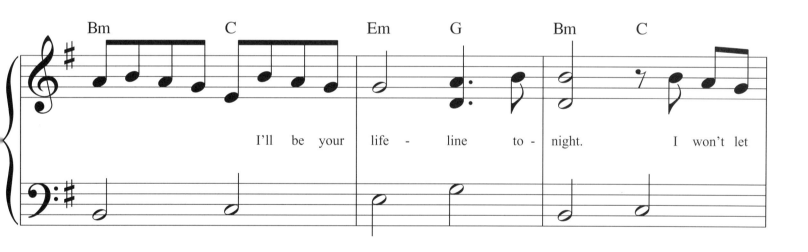

I'll be your life - line to - night. I won't let

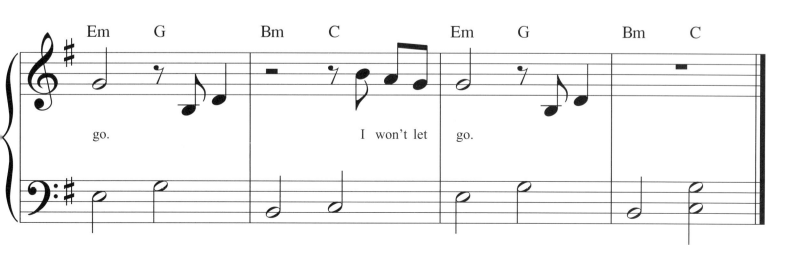

go. I won't let go.

DON'T WANNA KNOW

Words and Music by ADAM LEVINE, BENJAMIN LEVIN,
JOHN HENRY RYAN, AMMAR MALIK, JACOB KASHER HINDLIN,
ALEX BEN-ABDALLAH, KENDRICK LAMAR, KURTIS McKENZIE
and JON MILLS

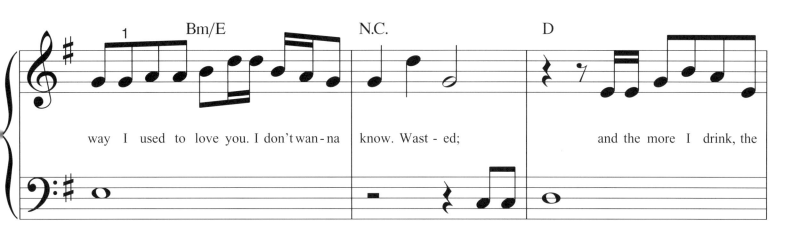

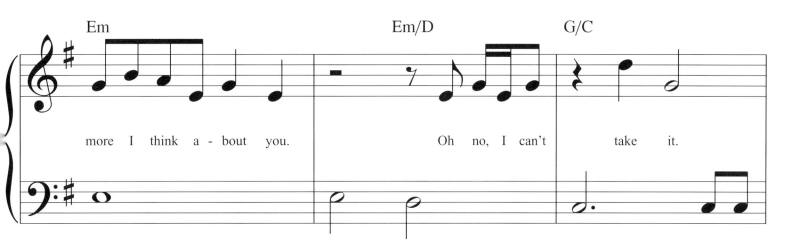

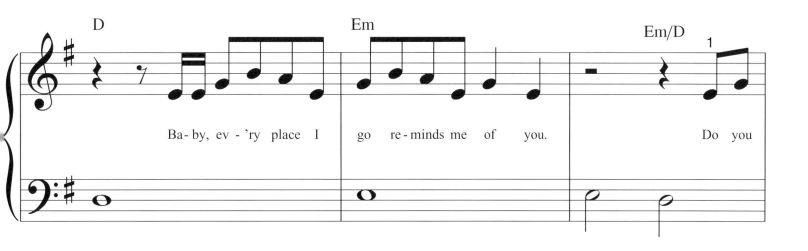

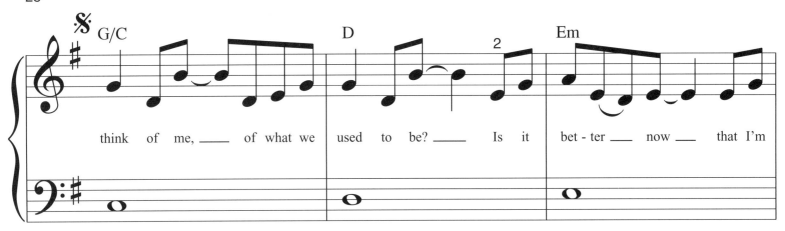

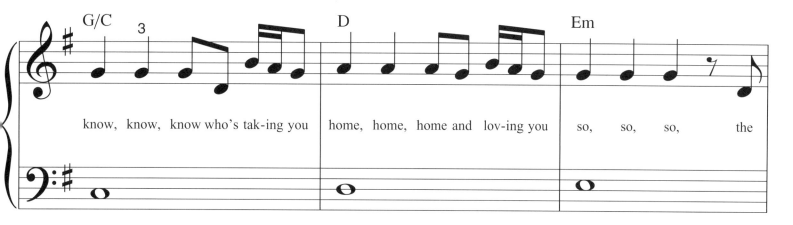

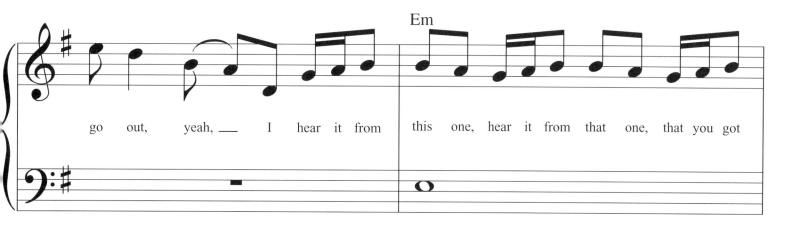

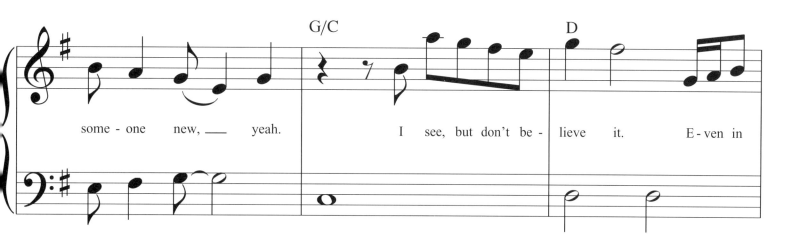

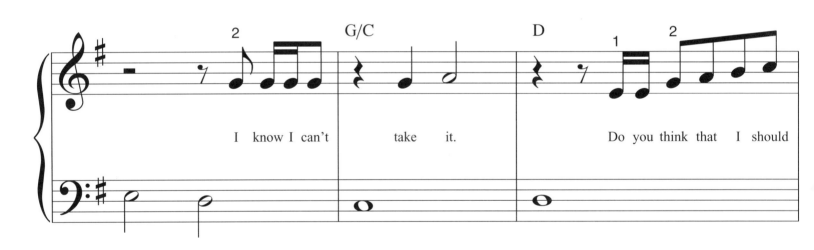

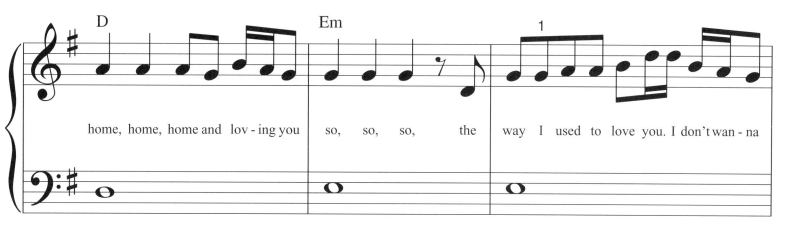

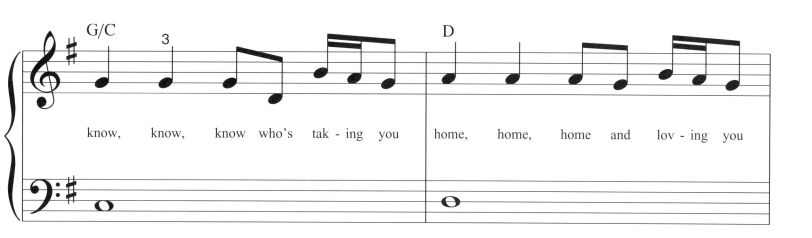

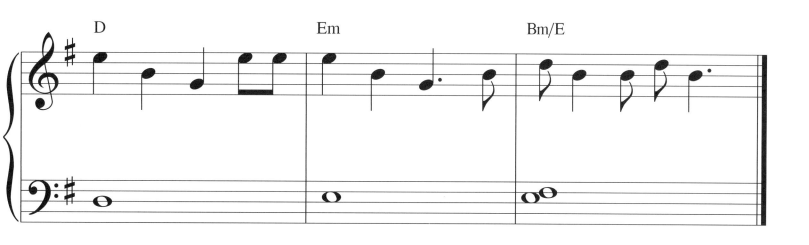

HANDCLAP

Words and Music by ERIC FREDERIC, SAMUEL HOLLANDER,
MICHAEL FITZPATRICK, JOSEPH KARNES, JAMES KING,
JEREMY RUZUMNA, NOELLE SCAGGS and JOHN WICKS

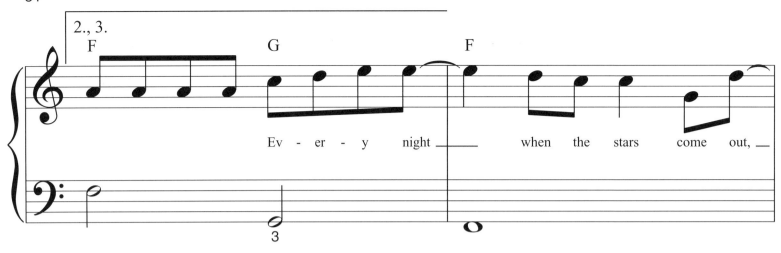

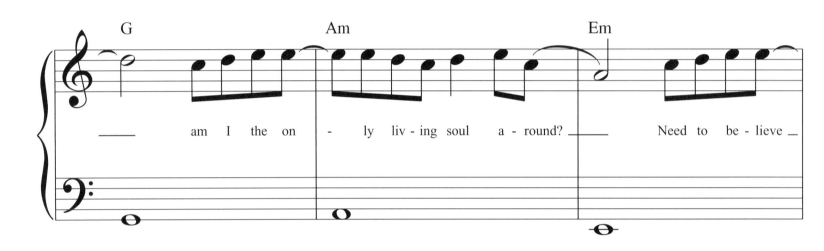

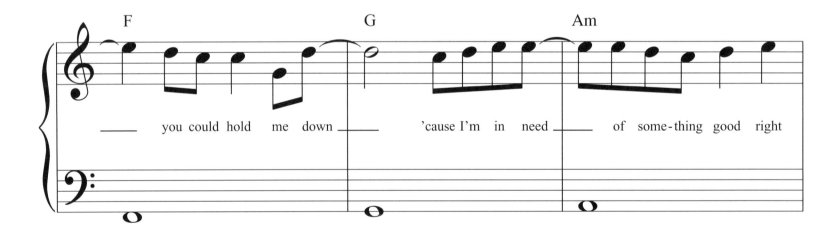

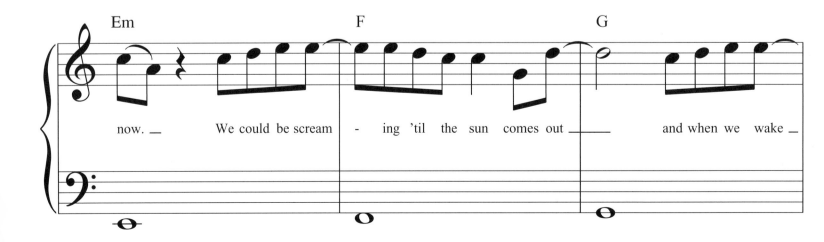

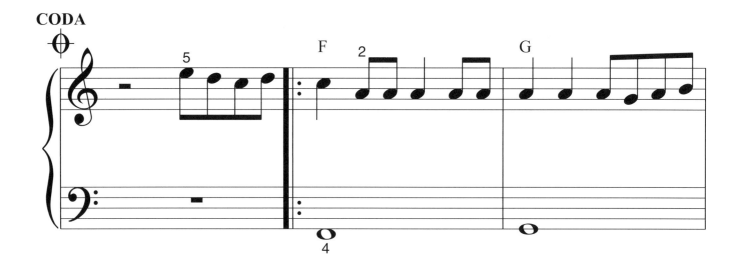

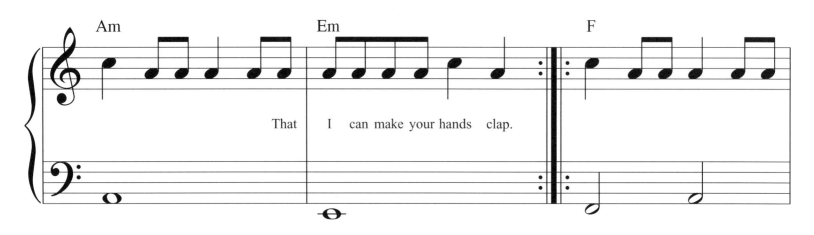

That I can make your hands clap.

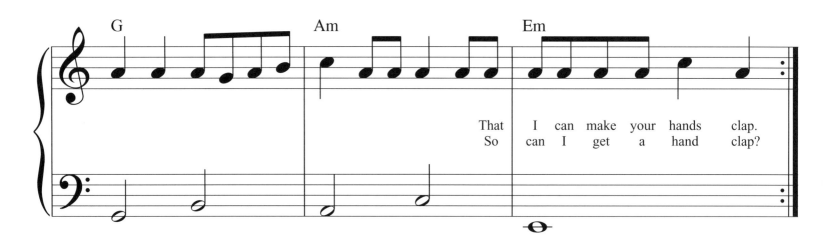

That I can make your hands clap.
So can I get a hand clap?

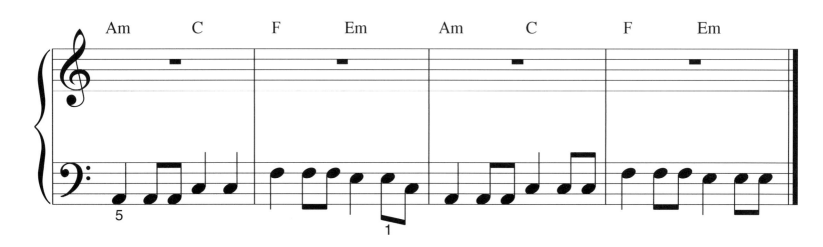

MILLION REASONS

Words and Music by STEFANI GERMANOTTA,
MARK RONSON and HILLARY LINDSEY

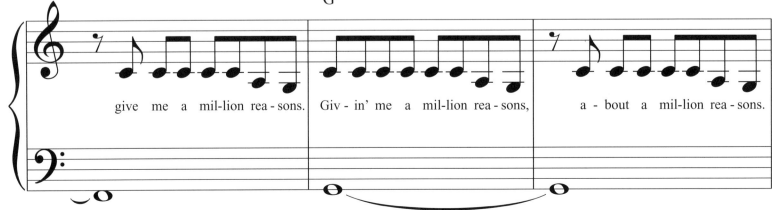

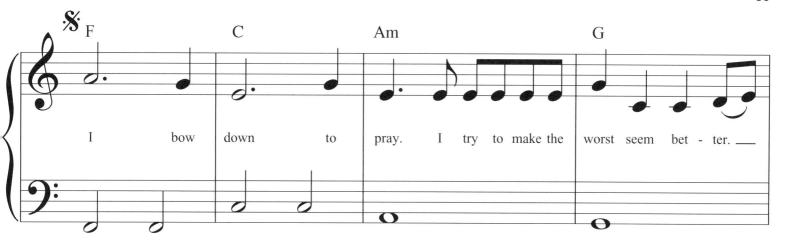

I bow down to pray. I try to make the worst seem bet - ter. ___

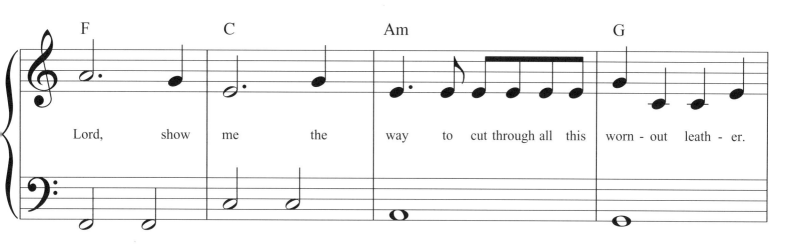

Lord, show me the way to cut through all this worn - out leath - er.

To Coda ⊕

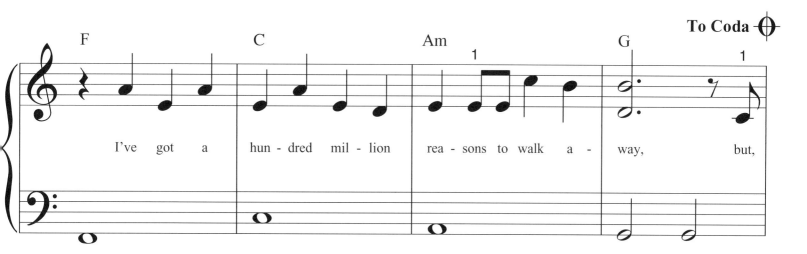

I've got a hun - dred mil - lion rea - sons to walk a - way, but,

ba - by, I just need one good one ___ to stay. ___

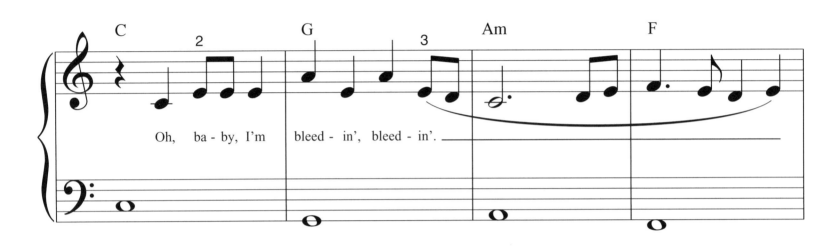

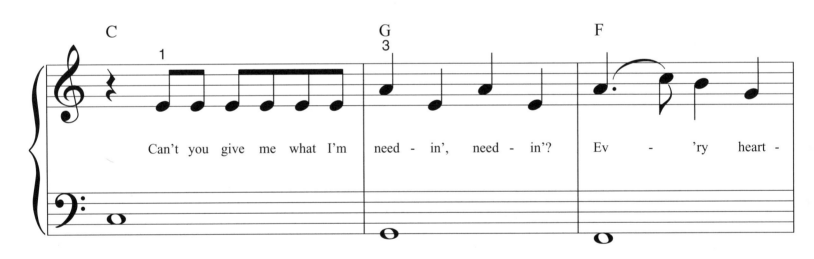

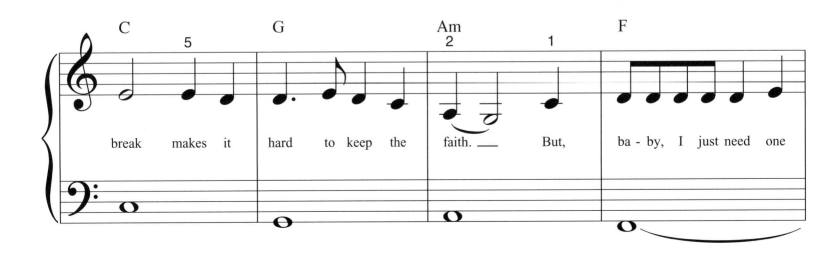

HEATHENS
from SUICIDE SQUAD

Words and Music by
TYLER JOSEPH

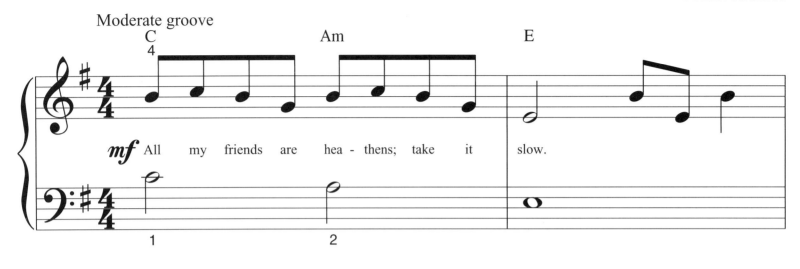

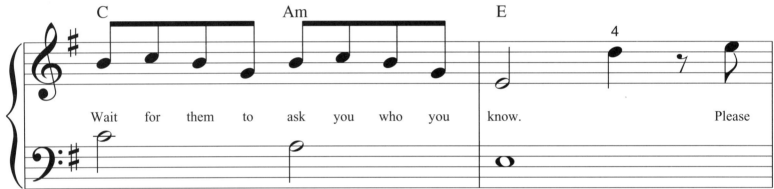

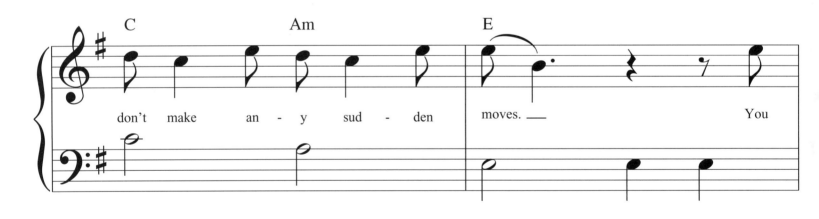

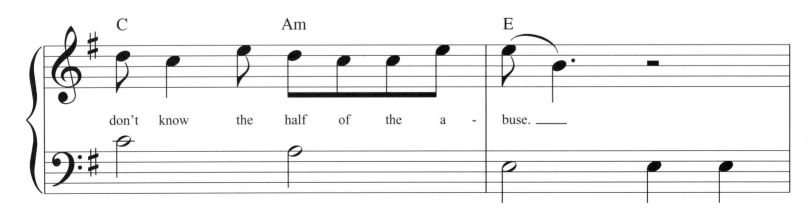

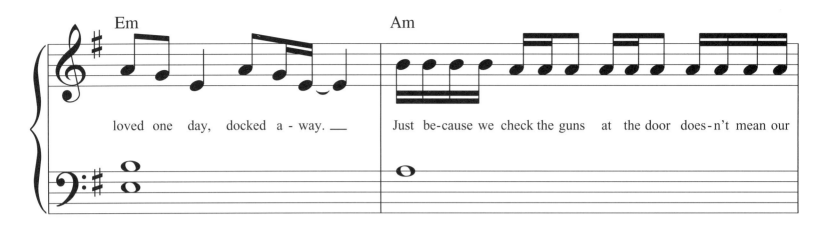

loved one day, docked a - way. ___ Just be-cause we check the guns at the door does-n't mean our

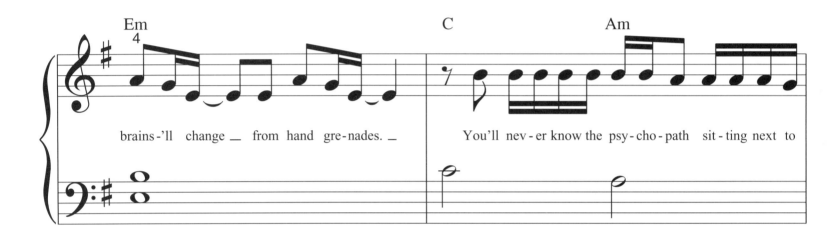

brains-'ll change ___ from hand gre-nades. ___ You'll nev-er know the psy-cho-path sit-ting next to

you. You'll nev-er know the mur-der-er sit-ting next to you. You'll think, "How'd I get here, sit-ting next to

D.S. al Coda

you?" But af-ter all I've said, please don't for - get.

CODA

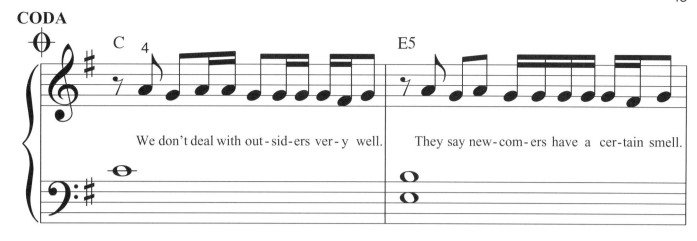

We don't deal with out-sid-ers ver-y well. They say new-com-ers have a cer-tain smell.

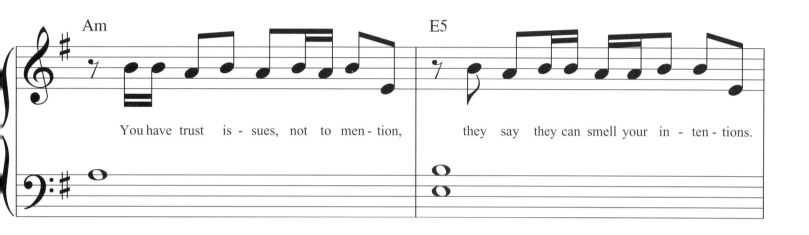

You have trust is - sues, not to men - tion, they say they can smell your in - ten - tions.

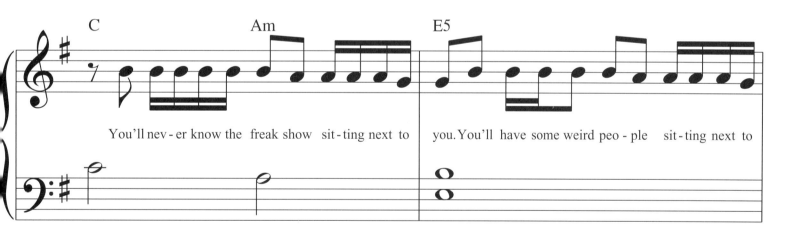

You'll nev - er know the freak show sit-ting next to you. You'll have some weird peo - ple sit-ting next to

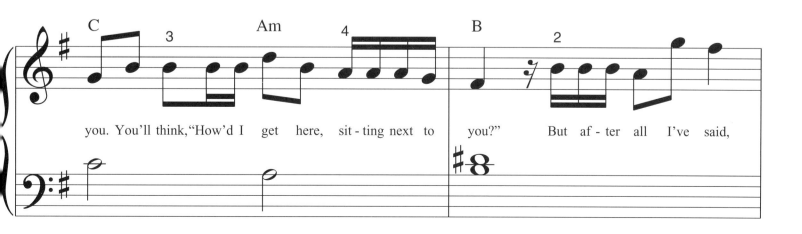

you. You'll think, "How'd I get here, sit - ting next to you?" But af - ter all I've said,

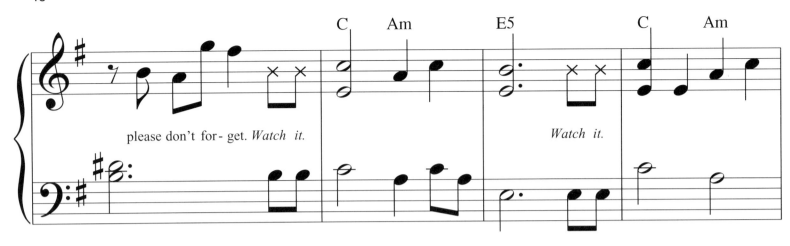

please don't for-get. *Watch it.* *Watch it.*

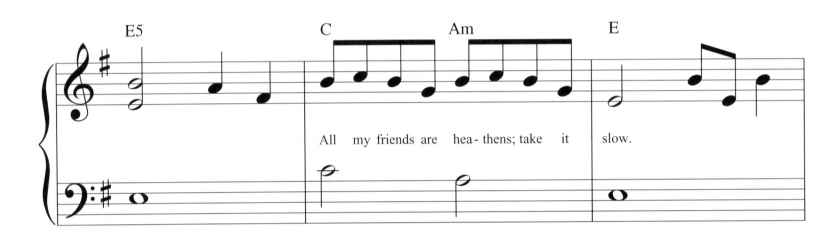

All my friends are hea-thens; take it slow.

Wait for them to ask you who you know. Please don't make an-y sud-den

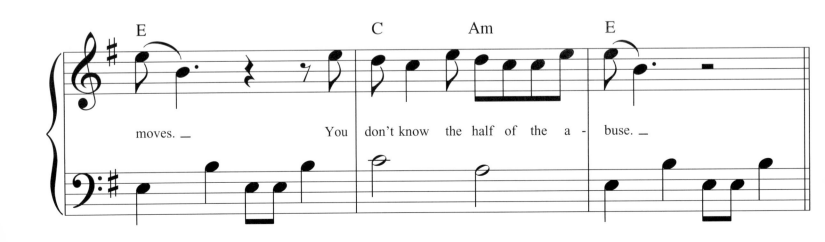

moves. — You don't know the half of the a-buse. —

I DON'T WANNA LIVE FOREVER
(Fifty Shades Darker)
from FIFTY SHADES DARKER

Words and Music by TAYLOR SWIFT,
JACK ANTONOFF and SAM DEW

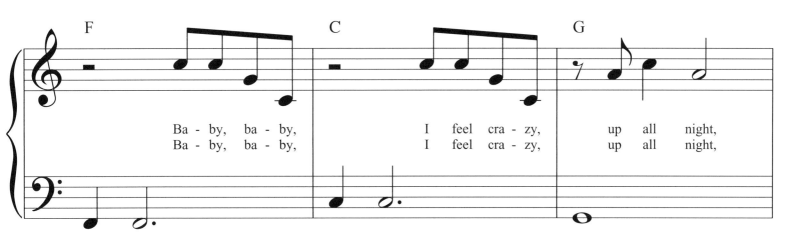

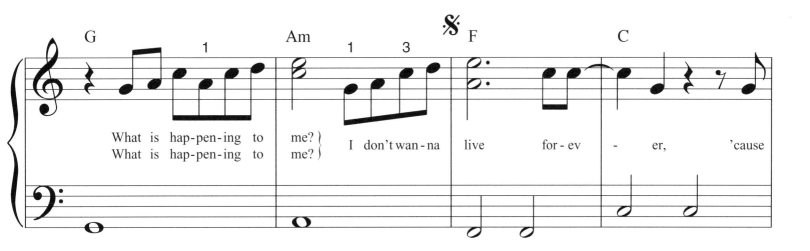

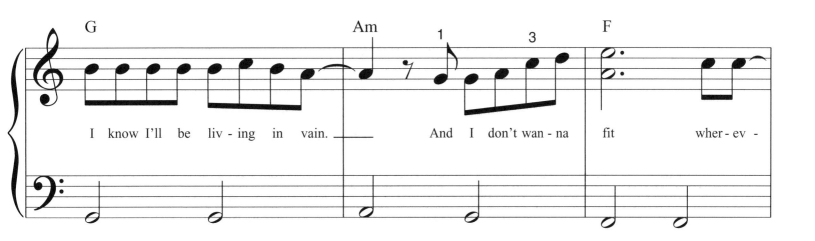

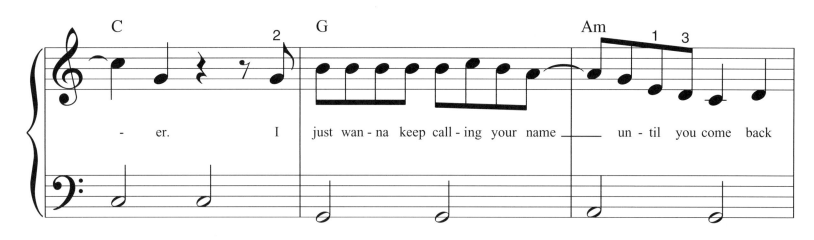

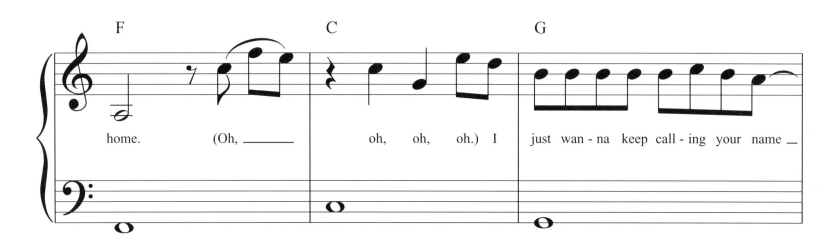

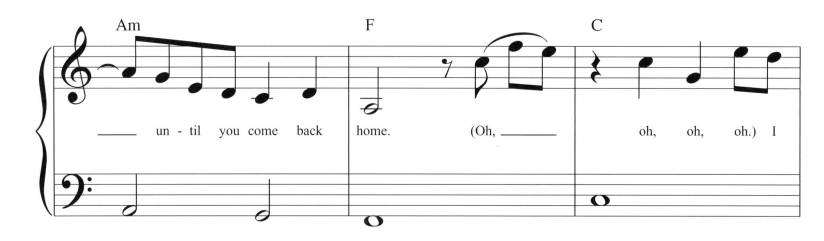

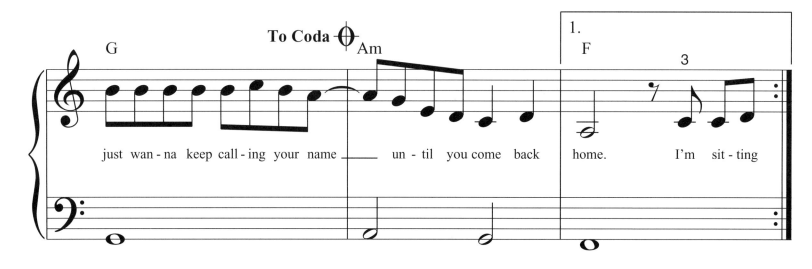

Now I'm in a cab; I tell him where your place is.

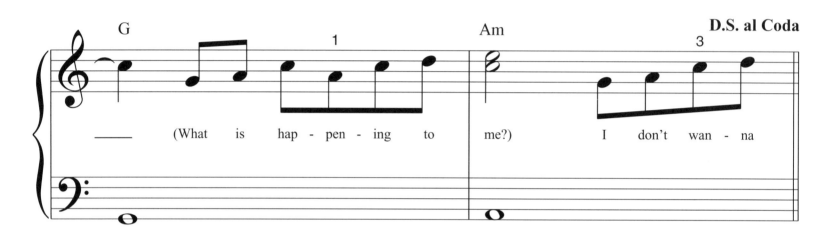

D.S. al Coda

—— (What is hap - pen - ing to me?) I don't wan - na

CODA

—— un - til you come back home. (Oh, —— oh, oh, oh.) I

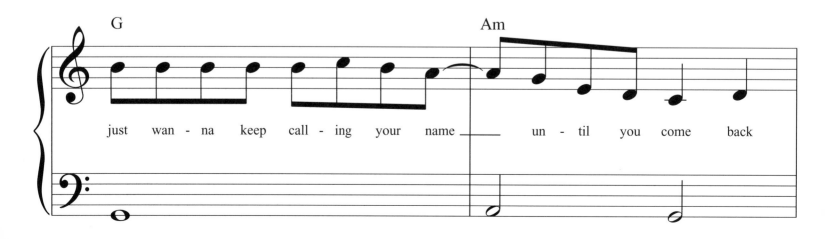

just wan - na keep call - ing your name —— un - til you come back

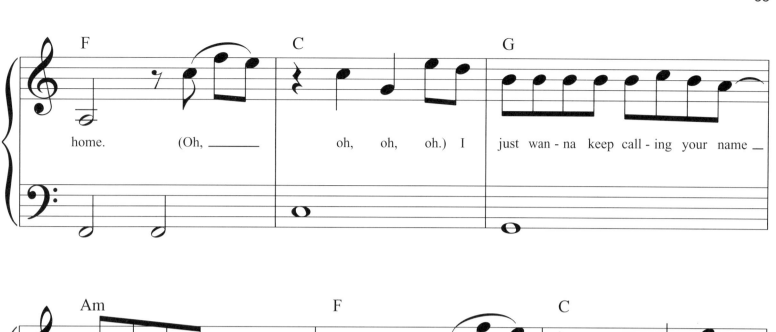

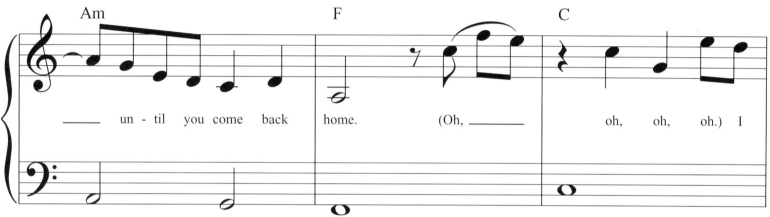

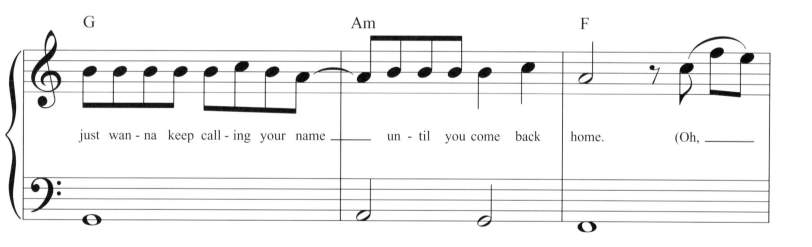

LOVE ON THE WEEKEND

Words and Music by
JOHN MAYER

It's a Fri - day;
You be the D. J.,

we fi - n'lly made it.
I'll be the driv - er.

I can't be - lieve I get to
You put your feet up in the

see ___ your face. ___
get - a - way car. ___

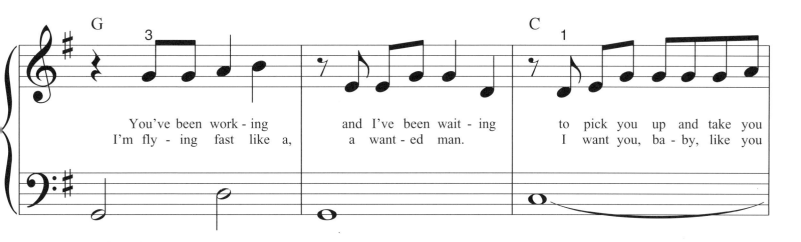

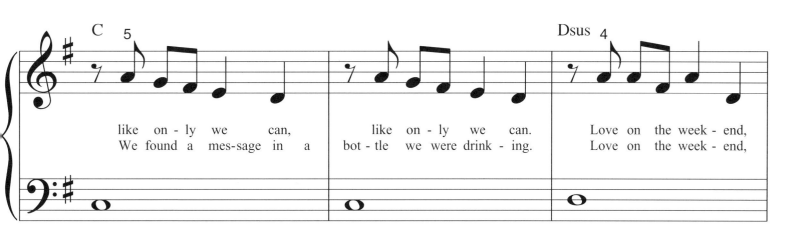

it's gon - na hurt me. My clothes are dirt - y and my friends are get - ting wor - ried.

Down there be - low us, un - der the clouds, ba - by, take my hand and pull me

down, down, down, down. And I'll be dream-ing of the next time we can go ___

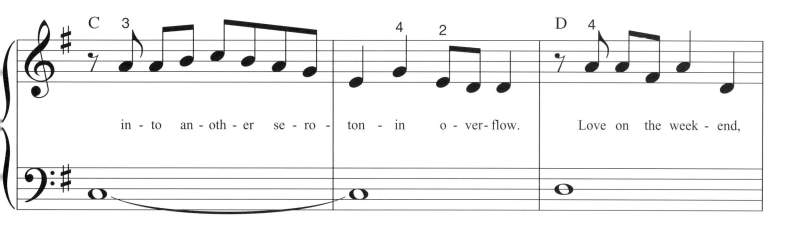

in - to an - oth - er se - ro - ton - in o - ver-flow. Love on the week - end,

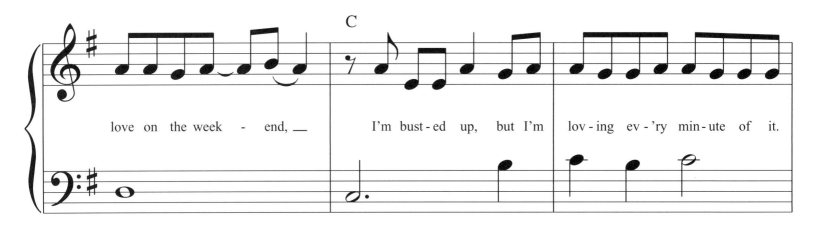

love on the week - end, ___ I'm bust-ed up, but I'm lov-ing ev-'ry min-ute of it.

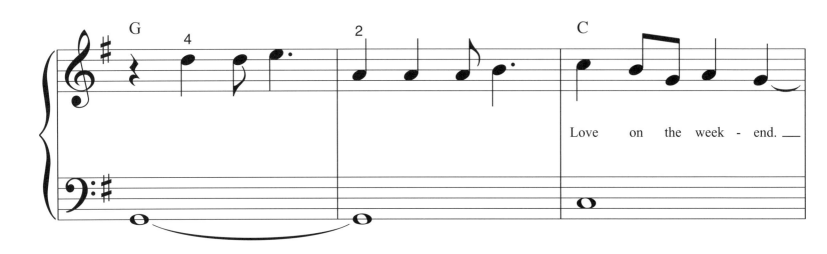

Love on the week - end. ___

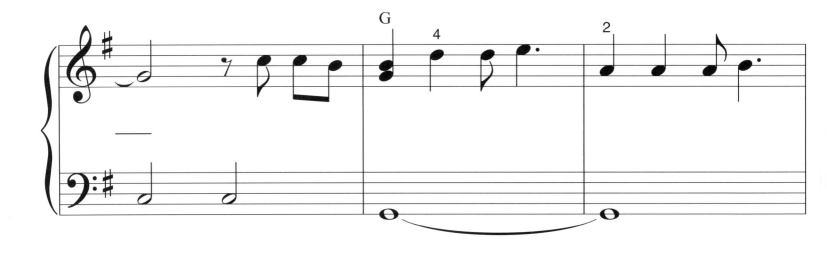

Love on the week - end. ___

SCARS TO YOUR BEAUTIFUL

Words and Music by ALESSIA CARACCIOLO,
WARREN FELDER, COLERIDGE TILLMAN
and ANDREW WANSEL

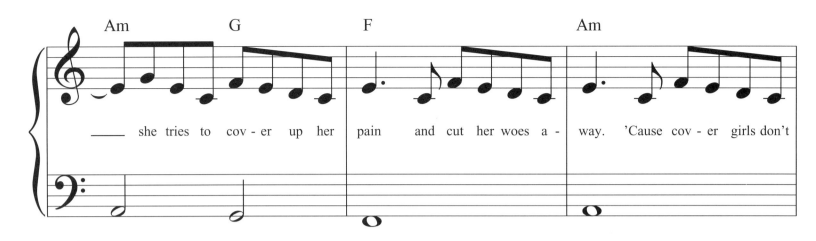

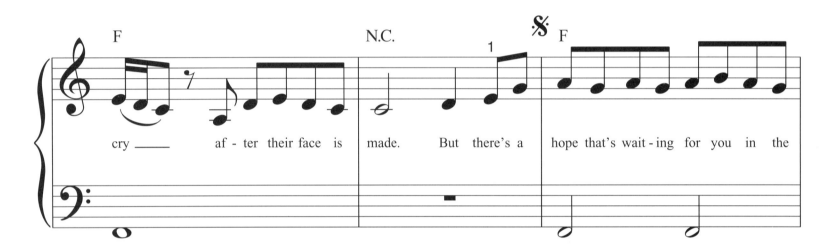

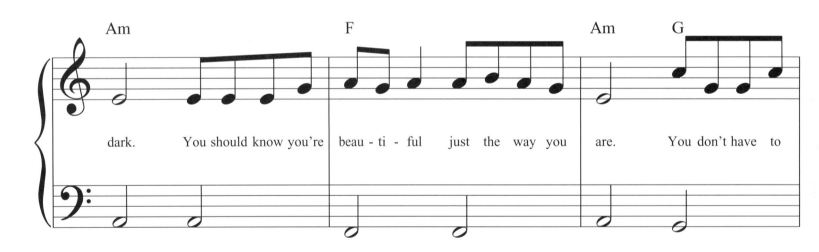

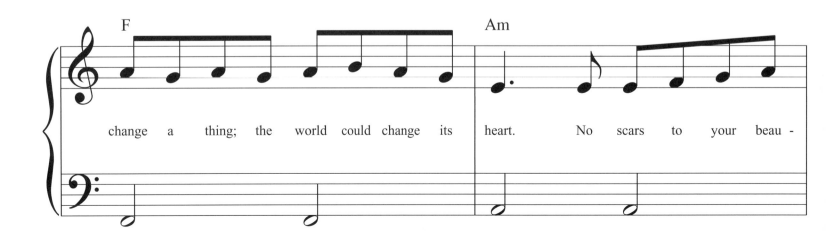

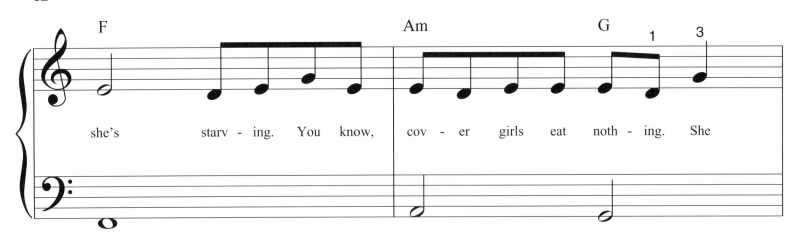

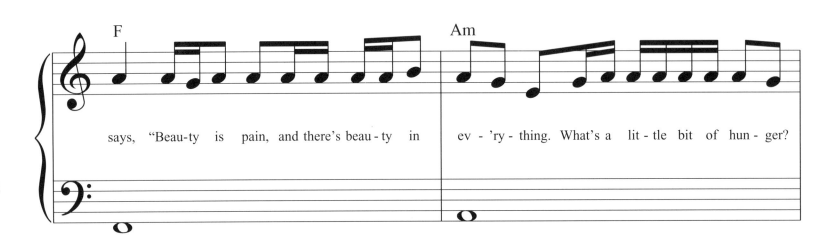

No bet-ter life than the life we're liv-ing. (No bet-ter life than the life we're liv-ing.)

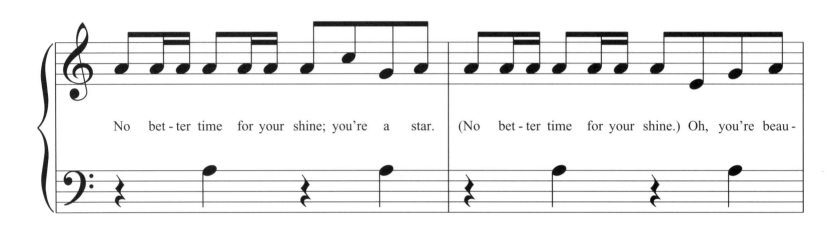

No bet-ter time for your shine; you're a star. (No bet-ter time for your shine.) Oh, you're beau-

ti - ful. _____ Oh, you're beau - ti - ful. _____ There's a hope that's wait-ing for you in the

dark. You should know you're beau-ti-ful just the way you are. You don't have to

SAY YOU WON'T LET GO

Words and Music by STEVEN SOLOMON,
JAMES ARTHUR and NEIL ORMANDY

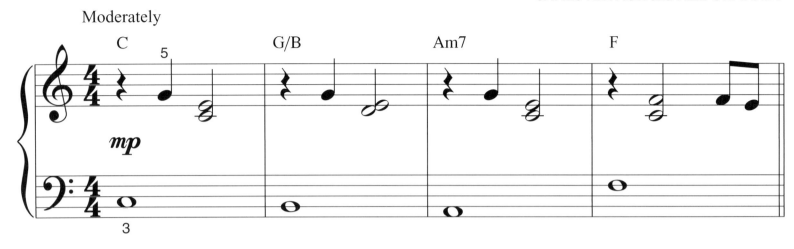

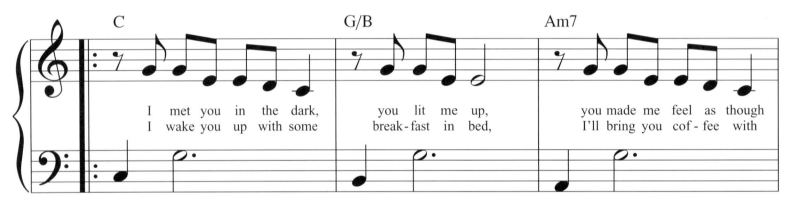

I met you in the dark, you lit me up, you made me feel as though
I wake you up with some break-fast in bed, I'll bring you cof-fee with

I was e-nough. We danced the night a-way, we drank too much,
a kiss on your head. I'll take the kids to school, wave them good-bye.

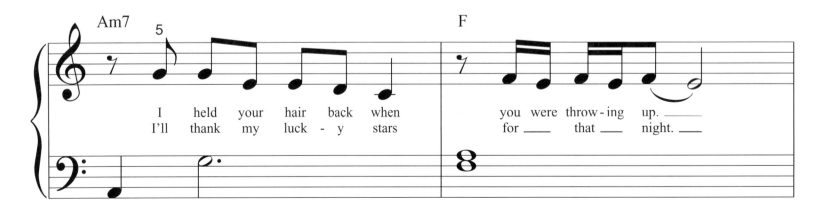

I held your hair back when you were throw-ing up.
I'll thank my luck-y stars for that night.

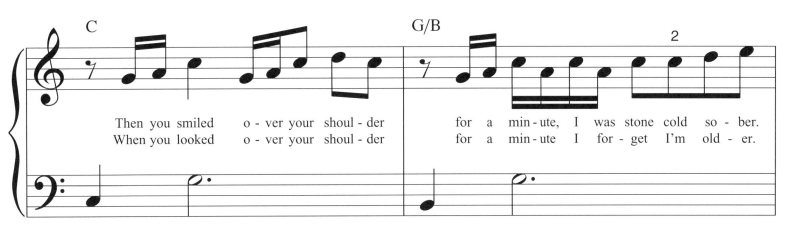

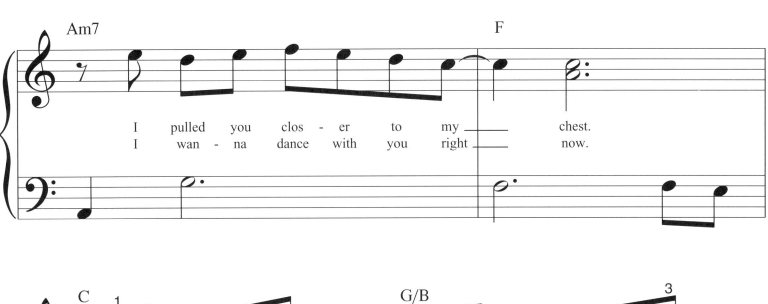

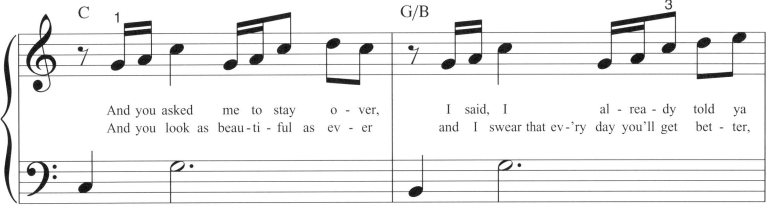

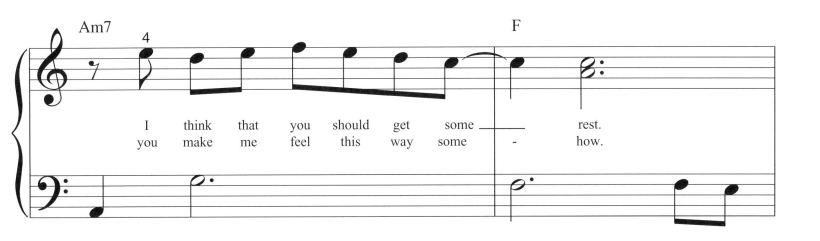

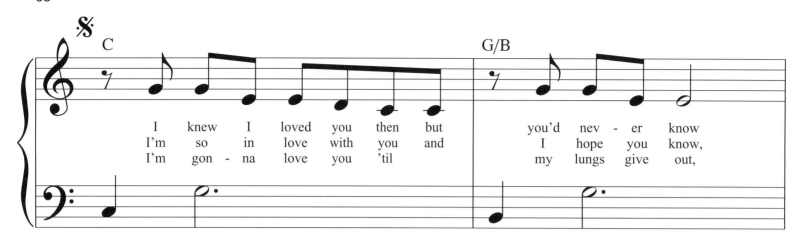

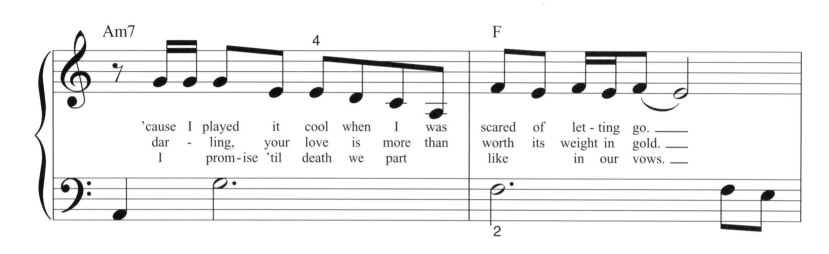

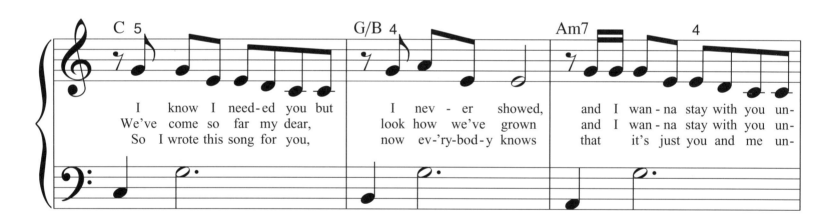

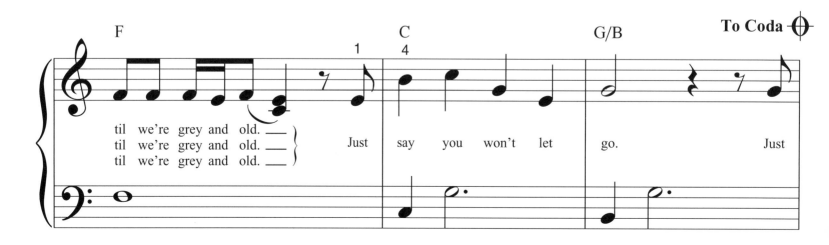

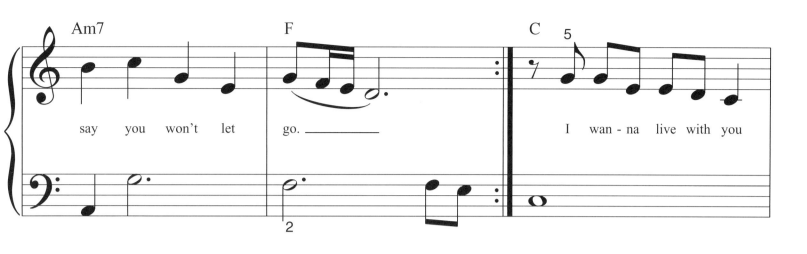

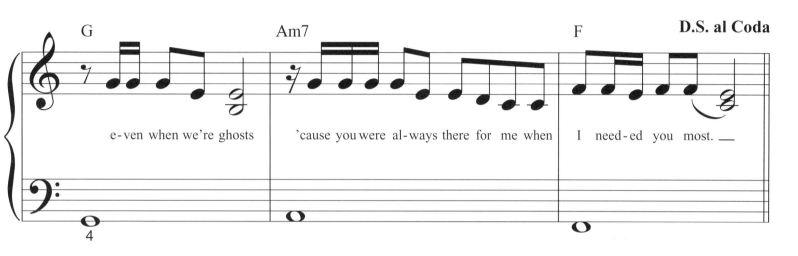

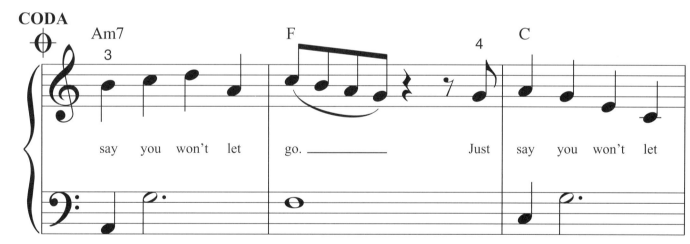

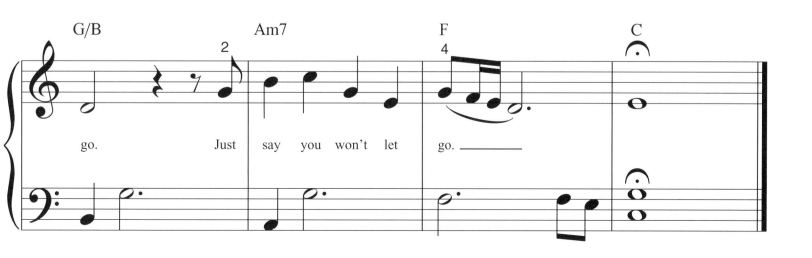

SEND MY LOVE
(To Your New Lover)

Words and Music by ADELE ADKINS,
MAX MARTIN and SHELLBACK

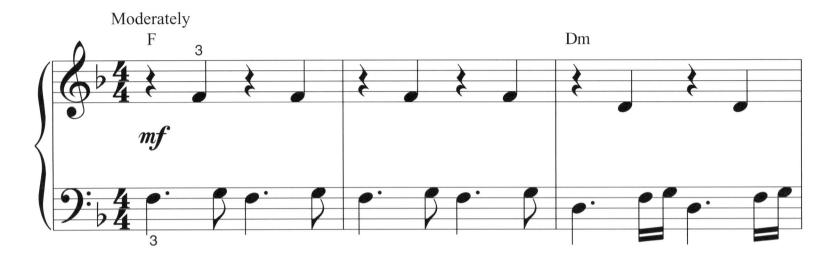

This was all you, none of it me,
I was too strong, you were trem-bling,

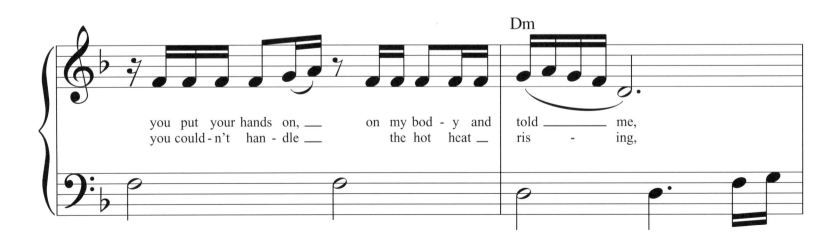

you put your hands on, on my bod-y and told me,
you could-n't han-dle the hot heat ris - ing,

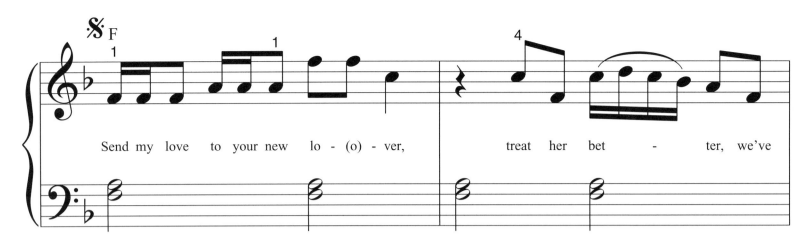

Send my love to your new lo - (o) - ver, treat her bet - ter, we've

got - ta let go of all of our ghosts, __ we both know we ain't kids no more. __

Send my love to your new lo - (o) - ver, treat her bet - ter, we've

To Coda

got - ta let go of all of our ghosts, __ we both know we ain't kids no more. __

If you're read-y, ___ if you're read-y, ___

if you're read-y, ___ I'm read-y. ___ If you're read-y, ___ if you're read-y, ___

we both know we ain't kids no more. ___ No, ___ we ain't kids no

more. ___

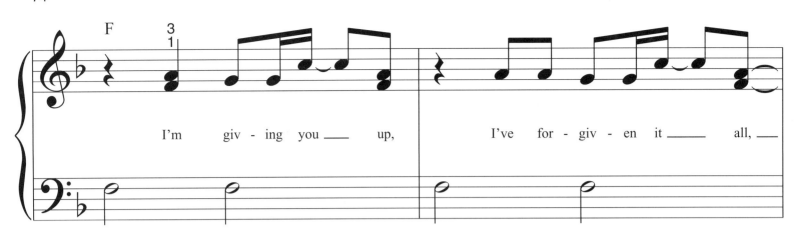

I'm giv-ing you ___ up, I've for-giv-en it ___ all, ___

D.S. al Coda

___ you set me free.

CODA

Send my love to your new lo - (o) - ver, treat her bet - ter, we've

got-ta let go of all of our ghosts, ___ we both know we ain't kids no more. ___

SHAPE OF YOU

Words and Music by ED SHEERAN,
STEVE MAC and JOHN McDAID

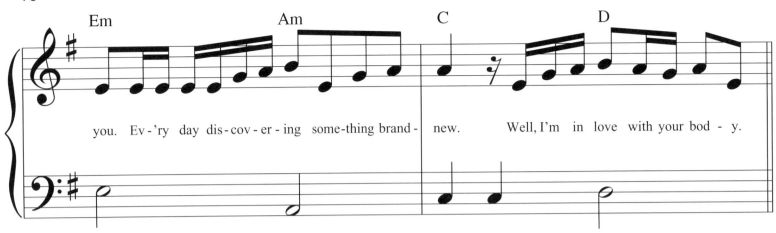

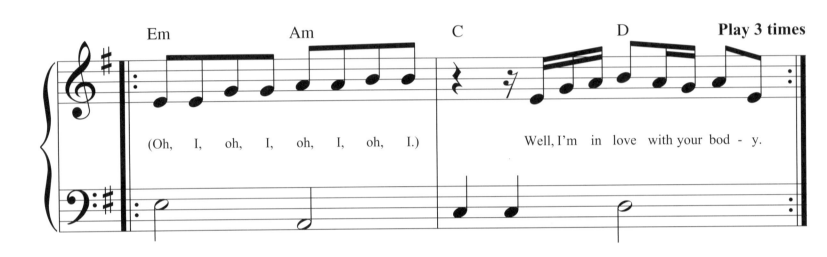

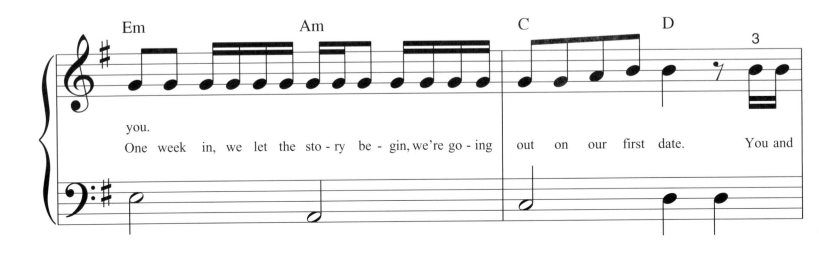

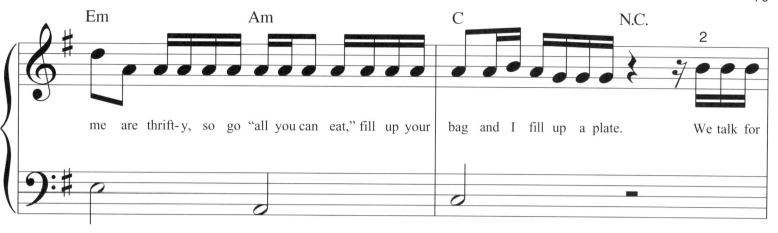

me are thrift-y, so go "all you can eat," fill up your bag and I fill up a plate. We talk for

hours and hours a-bout sweet and the sour, and how your fam-i-ly's do-ing o-kay, and leave and

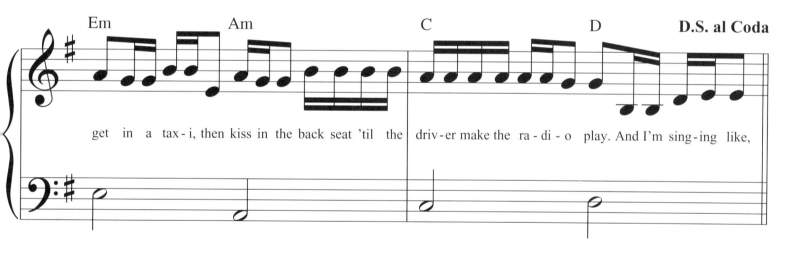

get in a tax-i, then kiss in the back seat 'til the driv-er make the ra-di-o play. And I'm sing-ing like,

D.S. al Coda

CODA

you. Come on, be my ba-by, come on. Come on, be my ba-by, come on.

Come on, be my ba-by, come on.

Come on, be my ba-by, come on.

Come on, be my ba-by, come on.

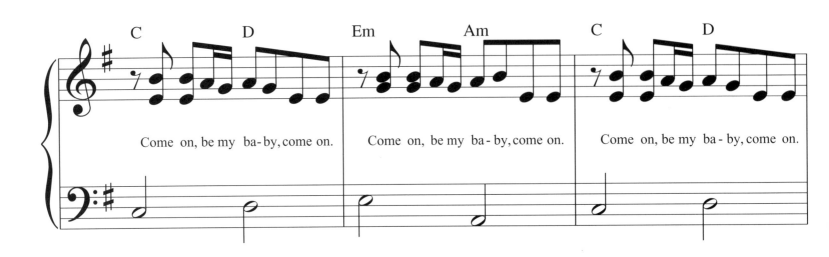

Come on, be my ba-by, come on.

Come on, be my ba-by, come on.

Come on, be my ba-by, come on.

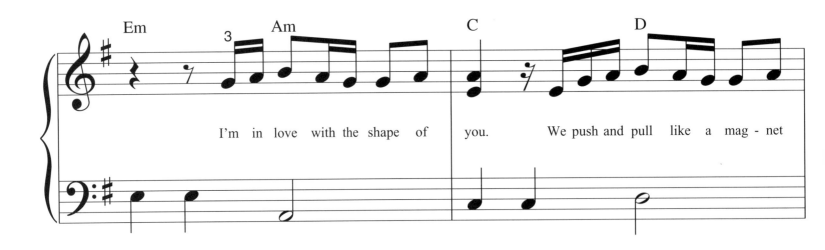

I'm in love with the shape of you. We push and pull like a mag-net

do. Al-though my heart is fall-ing, too, I'm in love with your bod-y. Last night you were in my

SIDE TO SIDE

Words and Music by ARIANA GRANDE,
ONIKA MARAJ, ALEXANDER KRONLUND,
MAX MARTIN, SAVAN KOTECHA and ILYA

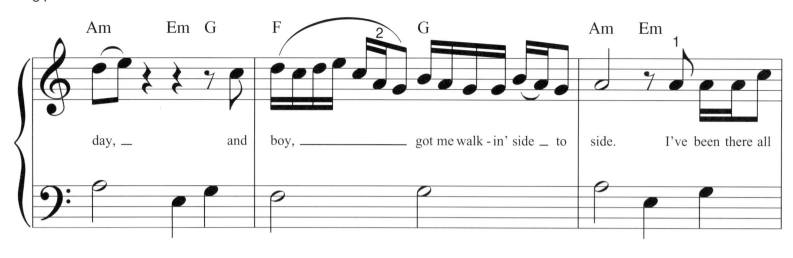

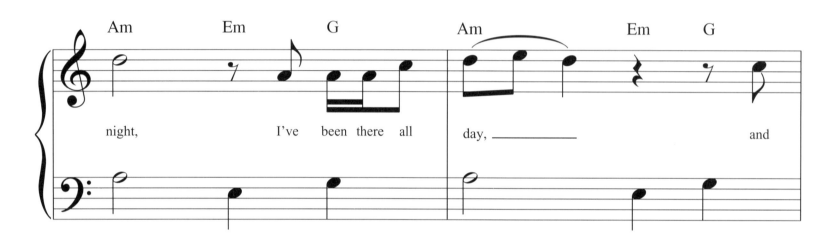

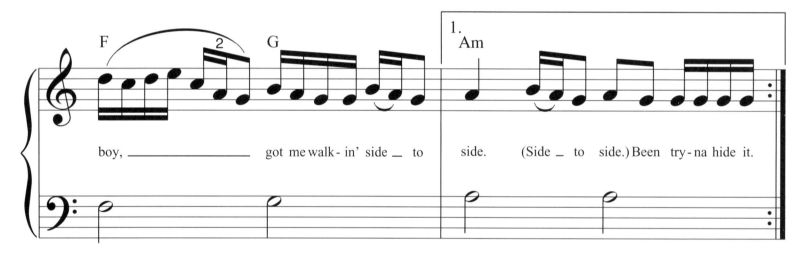

THIS TOWN

Words and Music by NIALL HORAN,
MICHAEL NEEDLE, DANIEL BRYER
and JAMIE SCOTT

If the whole world was watch - ing, I'd still dance with you; drive

high - ways and by - ways to be there with you. O - ver and o - ver, the

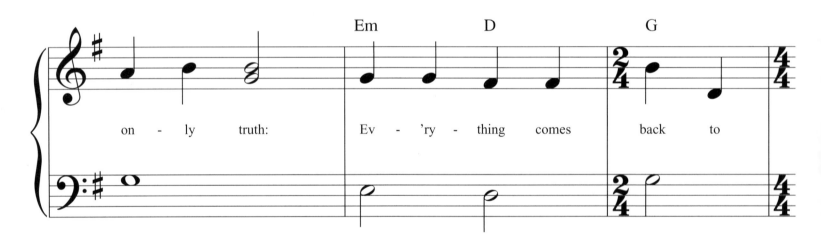

on - ly truth: Ev - 'ry - thing comes back to

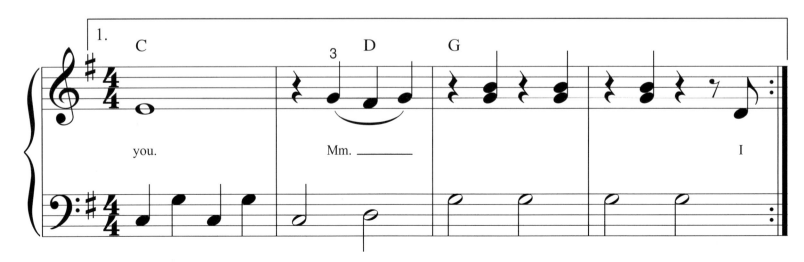

you. Mm. ____ I

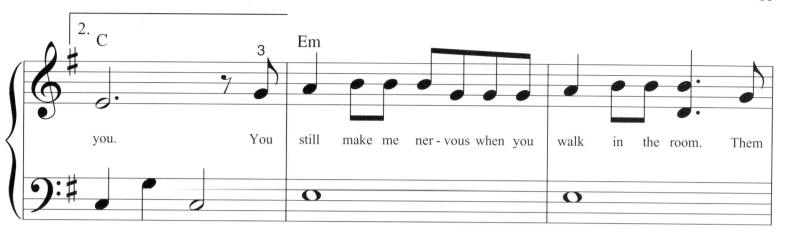

you. You still make me ner-vous when you walk in the room. Them

but-ter-flies, they come a-live when I'm next to you. O-ver and o-ver, the

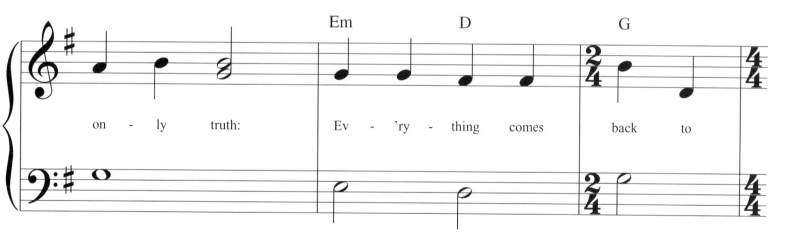

on - ly truth: Ev - 'ry - thing comes back to

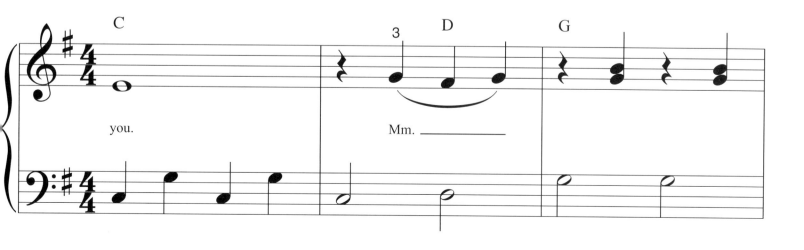

you. Mm. _____

And I know that it's wrong that I can't move

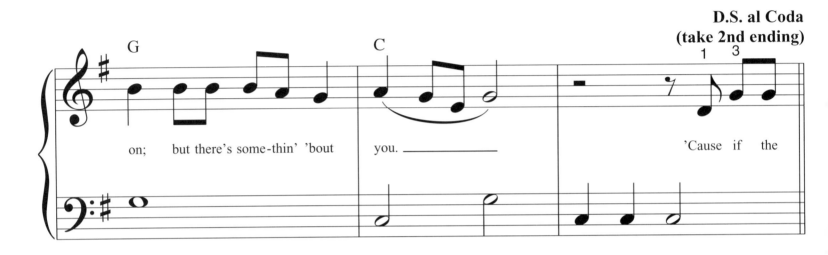

on; but there's some-thin' 'bout you. _____ 'Cause if the

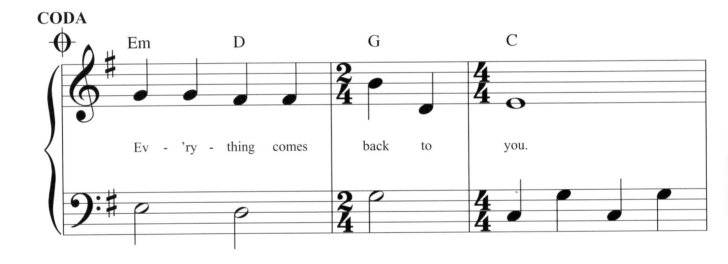

Ev - 'ry - thing comes back to you.

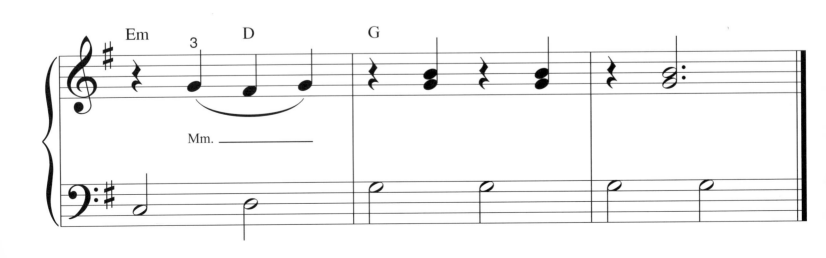

Mm. _____

24K MAGIC

Words and Music by BRUNO MARS,
PHILIP LAWRENCE and CHRIS BROWN

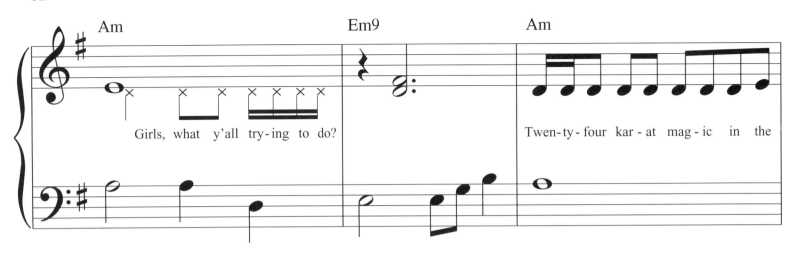

Girls, what y'all try-ing to do?

Twen-ty-four kar-at mag-ic in the

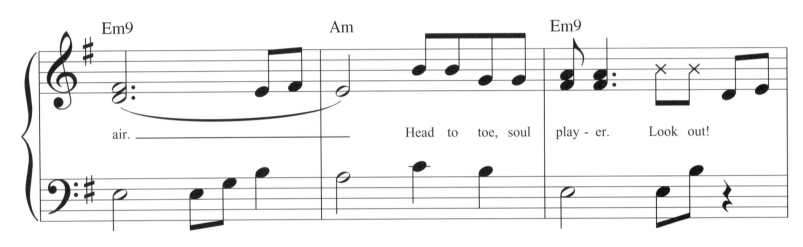

air. _____ Head to toe, soul play-er. Look out!

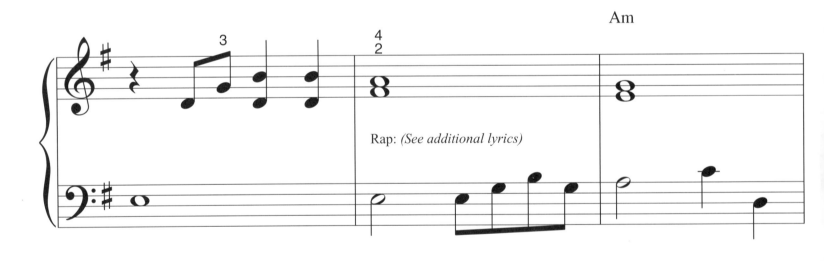

Rap: *(See additional lyrics)*

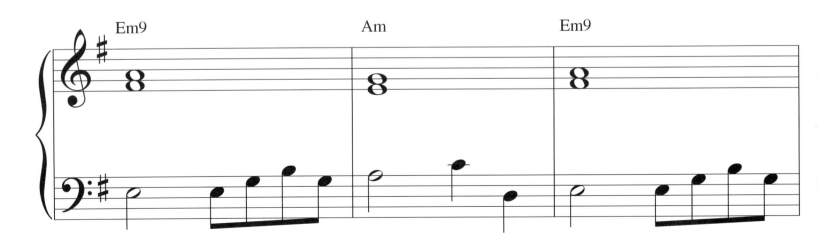

Put your pink - y rings up to the moon.

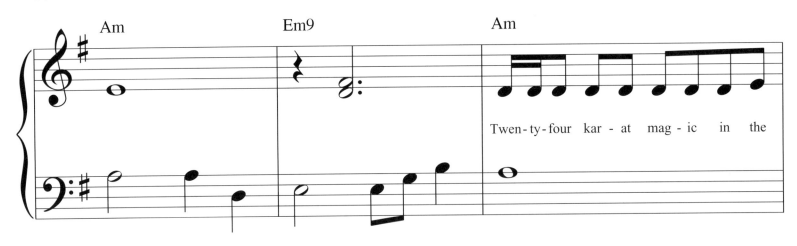

Twen-ty-four kar-at mag-ic in the

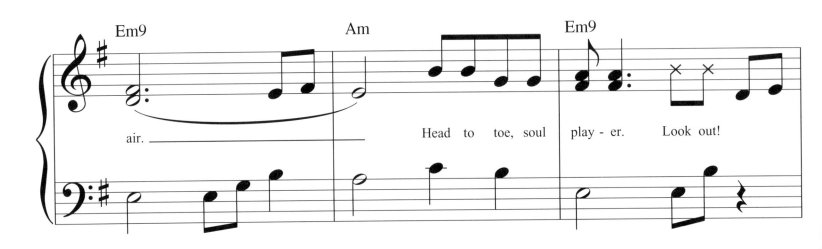

air. ___ Head to toe, soul play-er. Look out!

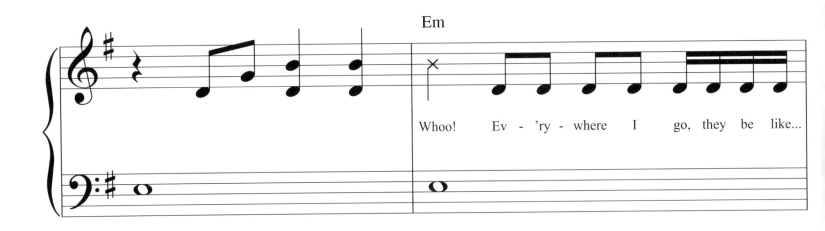

Whoo! Ev-'ry-where I go, they be like...

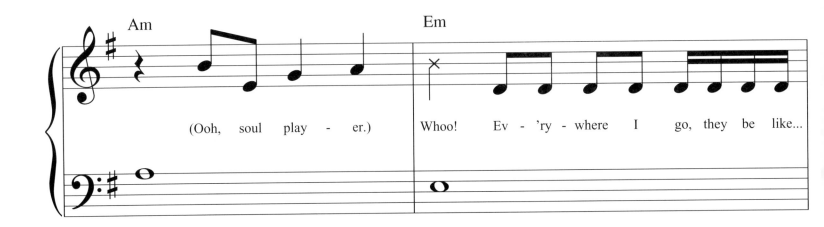

(Ooh, soul play-er.) Whoo! Ev-'ry-where I go, they be like...

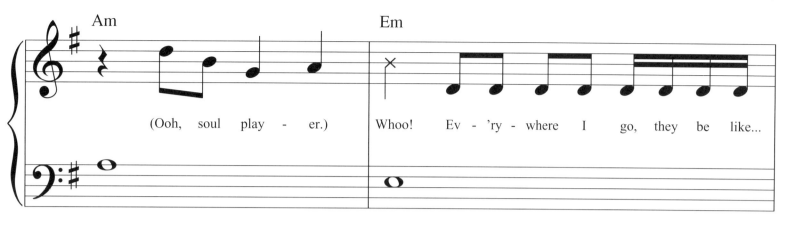

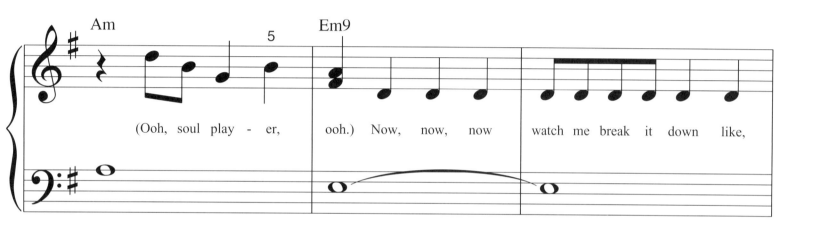

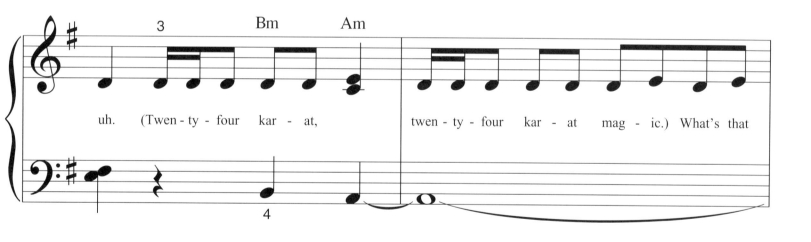

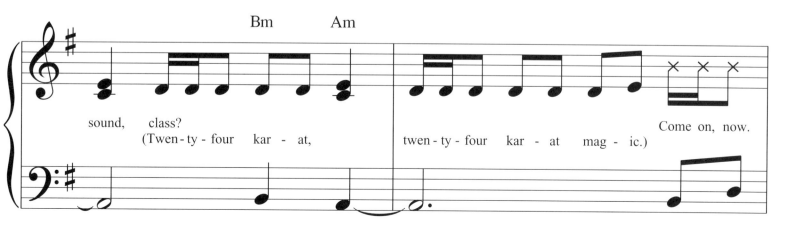

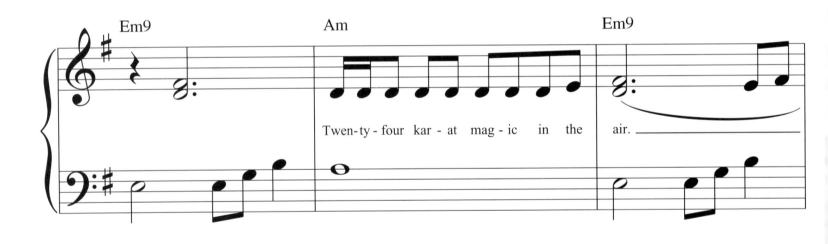

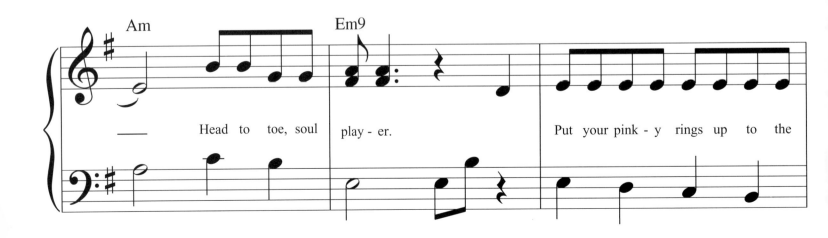

Additional Lyrics

Rap: Pop, pop, it's show time (show time,) show time (show time).
Guess who's back again.
Oh, they don't know? (Go on, tell 'em.)
They don't know? (Go on, tell 'em.)
I bet they know as soon as we walk in.
(Showin' up) wearin' Cuban links (yeah,) designer minks (yeah,)
Inglewood's finest shoes (whoop, whoop).
Don't look too hard; might hurt yourself.
Known to give the color red the blues.
I'm a dangerous man with some money in my pocket. (Keep up!)
So many pretty girls around me and they're waking up the rocket. (Keep up!)
Why you mad? Fix your face. Ain't my fault that y'all be jockin'. (Keep up!)
Players only, come on!

TREAT YOU BETTER

Words and Music by SHAWN MENDES,
SCOTT HARRIS and TEDDY GEIGER

see it on your face when you | say that he's the one that you | want. And you're
lov - ing that you're miss - ing. | Ba - by, just to wake up with | you would be

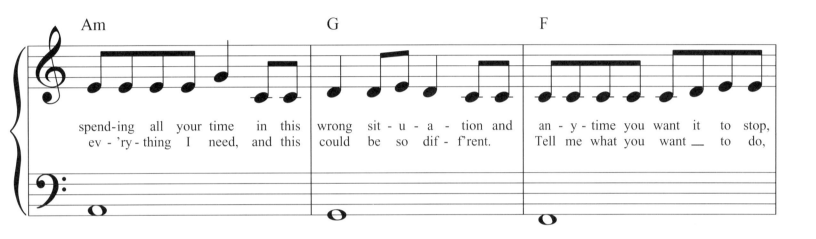

spend-ing all your time in this | wrong sit - u - a - tion and | an - y - time you want it to stop,
ev - 'ry - thing I need, and this | could be so dif - f'rent. | Tell me what you want __ to do,

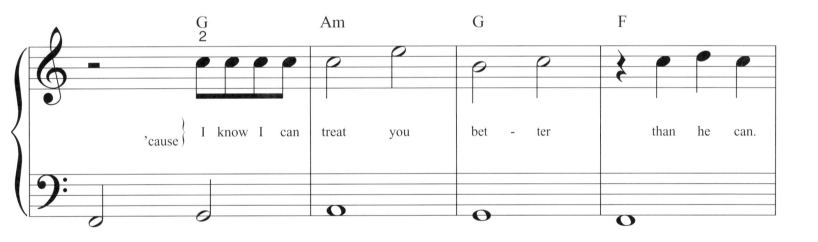

'cause I know I can treat you bet - ter than he can.

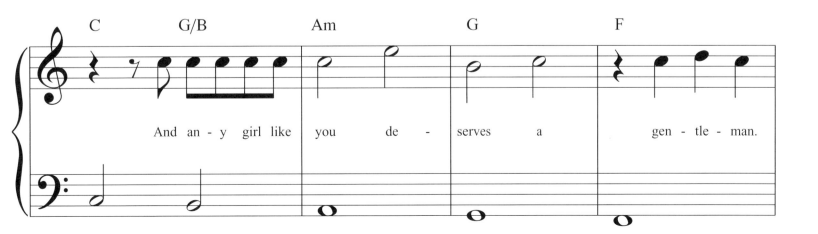

And an - y girl like you de - serves a gen - tle - man.

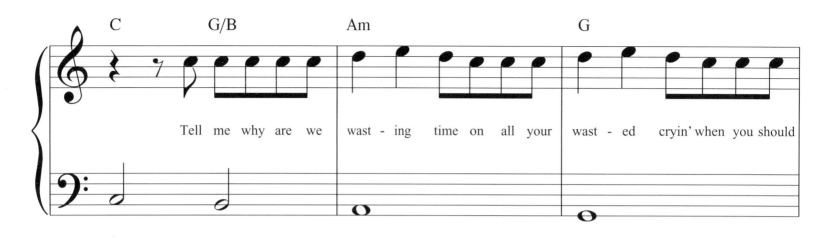

Tell me why are we wast - ing time on all your wast - ed cryin' when you should

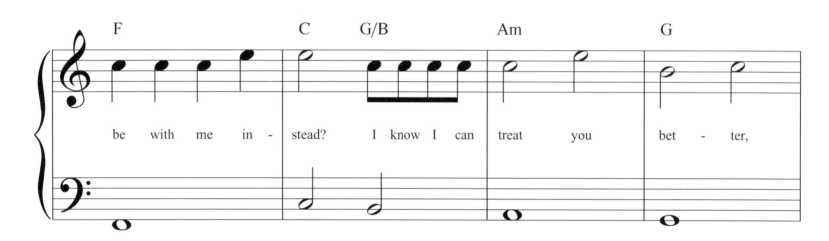

be with me in - stead? I know I can treat you bet - ter,

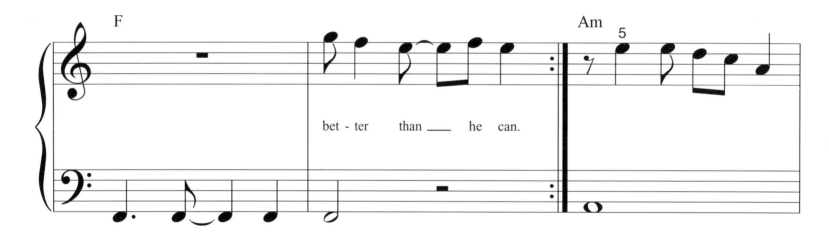

bet - ter than ___ he can.

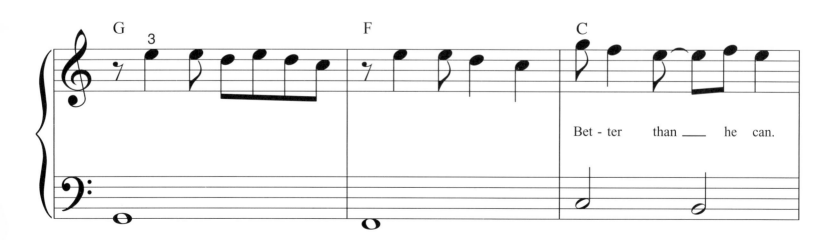

Bet - ter than ___ he can.

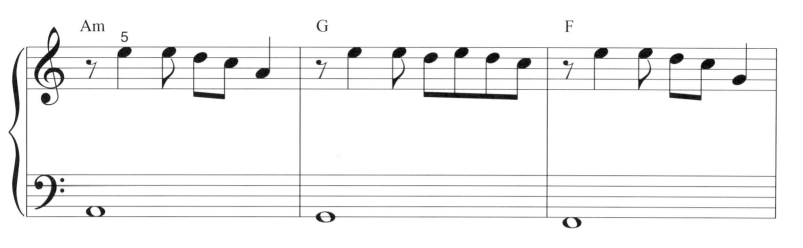

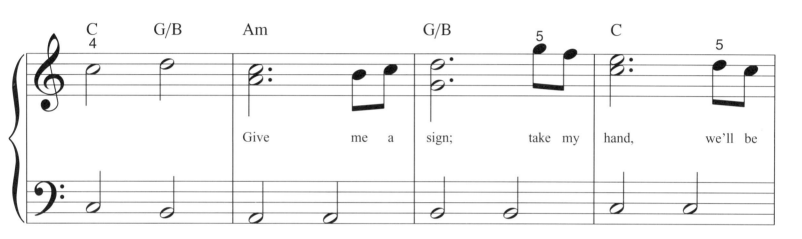

Give me a sign; take my hand, we'll be

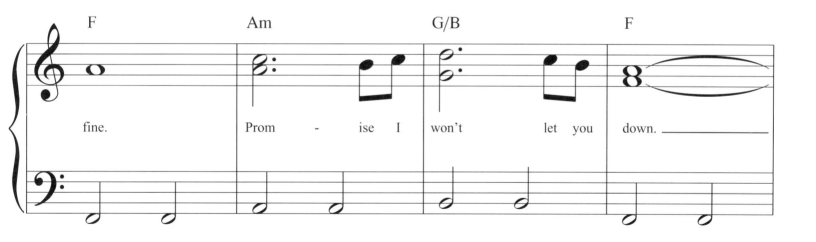

fine. Prom - ise I won't let you down. ____

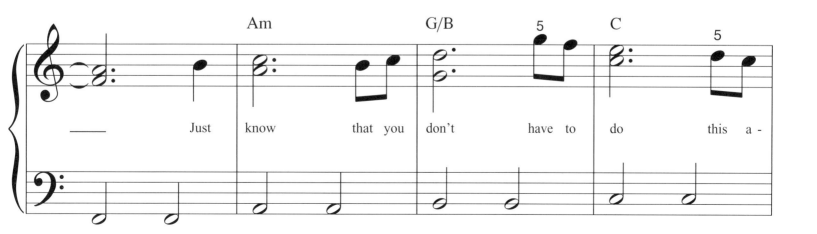

____ Just know that you don't have to do this a -

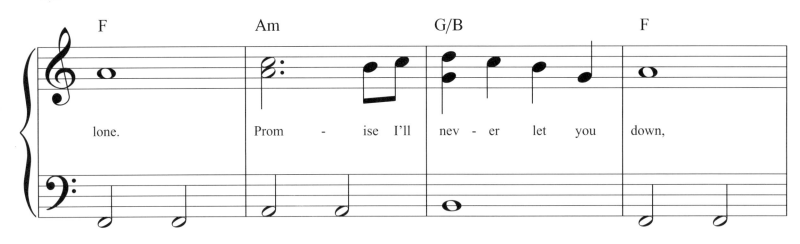

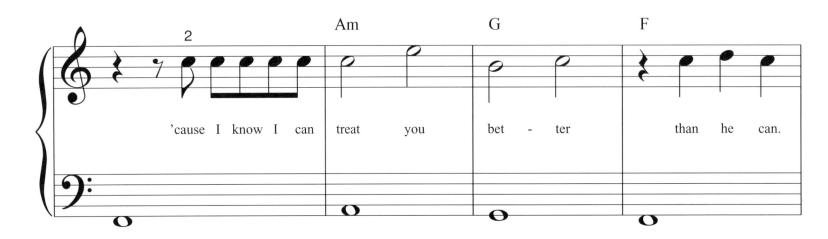

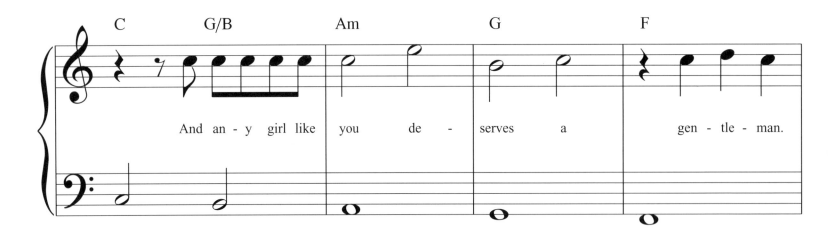

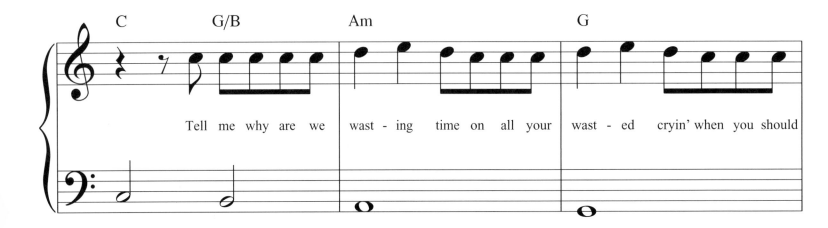

Big Fun with Big-Note Piano Books!

These songbooks feature exciting easy arrangements for beginning piano students.

Best of Adele

Now even beginners can play their favorite Adele tunes! This book features big-note arrangements of 10 top songs: Chasing Pavements • Daydreamer • Hometown Glory • Lovesong • Make You Feel My Love • One and Only • Rolling in the Deep • Set Fire to the Rain • Someone like You • Turning Tables.

00308601 ....$12.99

Beatles' Best

27 classics for beginners to enjoy, including: Can't Buy Me Love • Eleanor Rigby • Hey Jude • Michelle • Here, There and Everywhere • When I'm Sixty-Four • Yesterday • and more.

00222561 ....$14.99

The Best Songs Ever

70 favorites, featuring: Body and Soul • Crazy • Edelweiss • Fly Me to the Moon • Georgia on My Mind • Imagine • The Lady Is a Tramp • Memory • A String of Pearls • Tears in Heaven • Unforgettable • You Are So Beautiful • and more.

00310425.................................$19.95

Children's Favorite Movie Songs

arranged by Phillip Keveren

16 favorites from films, including: The Bare Necessities • Beauty and the Beast • Can You Feel the Love Tonight • Do-Re-Mi • The Rainbow Connection • Tomorrow • Zip-A-Dee-Doo-Dah • and more.

00310838.................................$12.99

Classical Music's Greatest Hits

24 beloved classical pieces, including: Air on the G String • Ave Maria • By the Beautiful Blue Danube • Canon in D • Eine Kleine Nachtmusik • Für Elise • Ode to Joy • Romeo and Juliet • Waltz of the Flowers • more.

00310475 ....$12.99

Disney Big-Note Collection

Over 40 Disney favorites, including: Circle of Life • Colors of the Wind • Hakuna Matata • It's a Small World • Under the Sea • A Whole New World • Winnie the Pooh • Zip-A-Dee-Doo-Dah • and more.

00316056 ....$19.99

Essential Classical

22 simplified piano pieces from top composers, including: Ave Maria (Schubert) • Blue Danube Waltz (Strauss) • Für Elise (Beethoven) • Jesu, Joy of Man's Desiring (Bach) • Morning (Grieg) • Pomp and Circumstance (Elgar) • and many more.

00311205 ....$10.99

Favorite Children's Songs

arranged by Bill Boyd

29 easy arrangements of songs to play and sing with children: Peter Cottontail • I Whistle a Happy Tune • It's a Small World • On the Good Ship Lollipop • The Rainbow Connection • and more!

00240251 ....$10.95

Frozen

9 songs from this hit Disney film, plus full-color illustrations from the movie. Songs include the standout single "Let It Go", plus: Do You Want to Build a Snowman? • For the First Time in Forever • Reindeer(s) Are Better Than People • and more.

00126105.................................$12.99

Happy Birthday to You and Other Great Songs for Big-Note Piano

16 essential favorites, including: Chitty Chitty Bang Bang • Good Night • Happy Birthday to You • Heart and Soul • Over the Rainbow • Sing • This Land Is Your Land • and more.

00119636.................................$9.99

Elton John – Greatest Hits

20 of his biggest hits, including: Bennie and the Jets • Candle in the Wind • Crocodile Rock • Rocket Man • Tiny Dancer • Your Song • and more.

00221832 ....$12.99

Les Misérables

14 favorites from the Broadway sensation arranged for beginning pianists. Titles include: At the End of the Day • Bring Him Home • Castle on a Cloud • I Dreamed a Dream • In My Life • On My Own • Who Am I? • and more.

00221812 ....$14.95

The Phantom of the Opera

9 songs from the Broadway spectacular, including: All I Ask of You • Angel of Music • Masquerade • The Music of the Night • The Phantom of the Opera • The Point of No Return • Prima Donna • Think of Me • Wishing You Were Somehow Here Again.

00110006 ....$14.99

Pride & Prejudice

Music from the Motion Picture Soundtrack

12 piano pieces from the 2006 Oscar-nominated film: Another Dance • Darcy's Letter • Georgiana • Leaving Netherfield • Liz on Top of the World • Meryton Townhall • The Secret Life of Daydreams • Stars and Butterflies • and more.

00316125 ....$12.99

The Sound of Music

arranged by Phillip Keveren

9 favorites: Climb Ev'ry Mountain • Do-Re-Mi • Edelweiss • The Lonely Goatherd • Maria • My Favorite Things • Sixteen Going on Seventeen • So Long, Farewell • The Sound of Music.

00316057 ....$10.99

Best of Taylor Swift

A dozen top tunes from this crossover sensation: Fearless • Fifteen • Hey Stephen • Love Story • Our Song • Picture to Burn • Teardrops on My Guitar • White Horse • You Belong with Me • and more.

00307143.................................$12.99

Worship Favorites

20 powerful songs: Above All • Come, Now Is the Time to Worship • I Could Sing of Your Love Forever • More Precious Than Silver • Open the Eyes of My Heart • Shout to the Lord • and more.

00311207 ....$10.95

Complete song lists online at
www.halleonard.com